Victorian Needlework

Techniques and Designs

Victorian Needlework
Techniques and Designs

Edited by Flora Klickmann

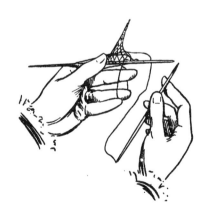

DOVER PUBLICATIONS, INC.
Mineola, New York

Bibliographical Note

This Dover edition, first published in 2002, is an unabridged republication of the work originally published in "The Home Art Series" by the Office of "The Girl's Own Paper & Woman's Magazine," London, n.d., under the title *The Cult of the Needle.*

Library of Congress Cataloging-in-Publication Data

Cult of the needle.
 Victorian needlework techniques and designs / edited by Flora Klickmann.
  p. cm.
 "An unabridged republication of the work originally published in 'The home art series' by the Office of the Girl's own paper & woman's magazine, London, n.d. under the title The cult of the needle"—Copr. p.
  ISBN 0-486-42154-6 (pbk.)
  1. Needlework. 2. Needlework, Victorian. I. Klickmann, Flora. II. Title.

TT750 .K6 2002
746.4'0941'09034—dc21

2002017449

Manufactured in the United States by Courier Corporation
42154603
www.doverpublications.com

THE
CULT
OF THE
NEEDLE

GIVING DIRECTIONS FOR
BULGARIAN, CATALAN,
HUNGARIAN AND BARO
EMBROIDERY, AMAGER
WORK, HEMSTITCHING,
NETTING, WOOL-WORK,
BOHEMIAN, CARRICKMA-
CROSS, INNISHMACSAINT
AND RETICELLA LACE,
AND OTHER FORMS OF
NEEDLECRAFT

Edited by
Flora Klickmann.

[Original book cover]

THE CULT OF THE NEEDLE

EDITED BY FLORA KLICKMANN.

The little squares here shown would make attractive d'oilies, or could be used as inlets in a larger piece of work. Many of the stitches used are similar to those in Hardanger work, and workers will easily follow them with the aid of the enlarged details given.

For this work use Congress canvas, with Peri-Lusta for the embroidery.

The little Star d'oily requires a 7-inch square of canvas. The work is commenced at the centre. When the centre is settled point out a little square of four threads and begin the work as the detail shows. The little triangles have 21 stitches, the larger covers 12, the shortest 4 threads; the 4 triangles make a square of 28 threads. The openwork squares around the triangles have 21 stitches on each side, the stitches cover 4 threads. When the squares are worked round, cut off the threads at the inside of the square as follows:—Cut away 4 threads on each side of corners, then leave 4 threads for weaving, and again cut away 4 threads on each side until you have 9 little squares in each square. The 4 threads you sew over and over as shown, and when

starting on the middle of each bar the thread should be looped and twisted to the other. For the outer solid portion every diamond is made of 23 stitches, the shortest covers 4, the longest 16 threads.

The Diagonal d'oily measures the same as the previous one. Here the work is also started at the centre. The squares are made by 21 stitches over 4 threads, 7 squares are to be worked diagonally across the linen. On each side of the squares the solid triangles already described should be made 12 on each side.

When finished, work along the triangles the little squares of 4 threads, 36 on each side. Then start at the 12th little square and form a large square on each side as shown, each square contained by 12 little squares. In the centre of the big square make a little square of 4 threads, having on each side 5 stitches over 4 threads. The star is made of 17 stitches on each diamond, the shortest 4, the longest 8 threads. The little diagram is made by 12 stitches, the shortest over 4, the longest over 12 threads.

The separate detail of this section

How to work Hungarian Embroidery

Hungarian Embroidery.

The open-work triangle used in the Diagonal D'oily.

shows a rather more elaborate diagram, composed of 20 stitches and having a cross-stitch in the middle. The triangle in openwork has on the outside 53 stitches over 4 threads. After outlining it, cut

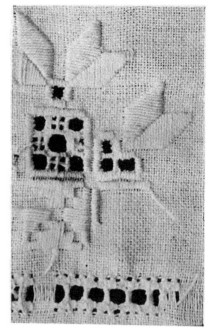

Details of the Star D'oily and the Insertion.

the threads as for Hardanger work, and work over and over the 4 threads each way that are left. For the openwork squares leave 4 threads in the middle of each side, cutting away the remaining threads, carry the working

Details of the Diagonal D'oily.

thread from corner to corner, and work over and over the bars formed.

The insertion requires a 3½-inch wide strip of linen. The stars are worked as for the d'oily. The triangle has 37 stitches on the straight side. Leave 4 threads below this straight side. Then draw out 1 thread. Again leave 4 threads, and draw 6 threads, leave 4 and draw 1. Each vertical stitch is taken over 4 threads, and the long bars are worked over 8 threads. This insertion would make a very handsome blouse trimming.

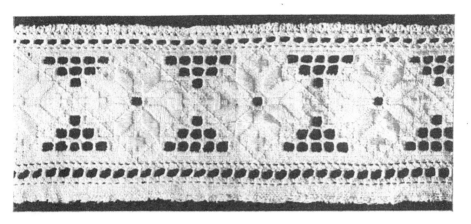

AN INSERTION DESIGN.

A HANDSOME DIAGONAL D'OILY.

The Making of Fringes.

AN EASILY-MADE FRINGE.

Knotted fringe, one of the many revived handicrafts, is coming very much to the fore. And no wonder—for it is one of the most graceful additions to pieces of stitchery. The rejuvenation of the craft is heartily welcomed by all who treasure some lovely old fringe from "great-grand-mamma's bottom-drawer." And everybody who

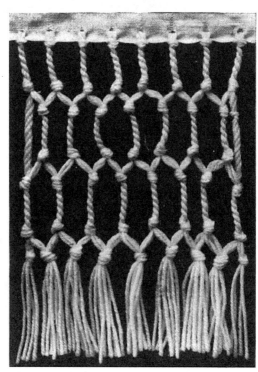

A TWINED FRINGE.

likes to turn out high-class workmanlike stitchery, will find in fringe-making not only a means of aiding materially to the beauty and value of her work, but also an art which offers large scope both for artistic taste and for manipulative skill.

The Origin of Fringes.

The original idea of fringe-making was to utilise the remnant of the warp. When a piece of material was finished in the loom, the last three-quarter yard of warp could not be filled in, as the machinery of the loom through which the warp was cunningly threaded hindered the shuttle from further work. However, it was found that the fringe looked pretty, and the idea to knot it came by degrees.

It may be mentioned here that this was the beginning of another art, the one which developed into "pillow-lace." But this is by the way.

To return to the practical point of the ques-

4

tion, knotted fringes are now made of various materials applied on the embroidery as well as by unravelling the weft and knotting the warp. In making it with the warp, the length and pattern should be decided upon before cutting out your material, and a piece of the material should be left free for the fringe. When the embroidery is finished, the woof should be unravelled, care being taken that the warp does not get too entangled. Remember that the knotting takes up a considerable length. It is advisable to allow an extra two-thirds, *i.e.*, if your fringe is to be 6 inches long the warp should be 10 inches, as the 4 inches will be taken up by the knots.

Knotting and Twining.

Before beginning to knot the fringe, secure the piece of tapestry by means of some heavy weights laid on it. Equalise your tassels as much as possible, and when practicable count the

threads of every tassel. (This can, of course, not be rigorously carried out when working on fine material). Make a knot on every "tassel," manipulating the knot with a bodkin or some such blunt implement. When the 1st row is knotted, every tassel should be equally divided, each half being joined on to the neighbouring half-tassel. The knot joining the 2 halves together is done as described above.

One variation is to twine 1 row: Divide tassel, twine tightly and the

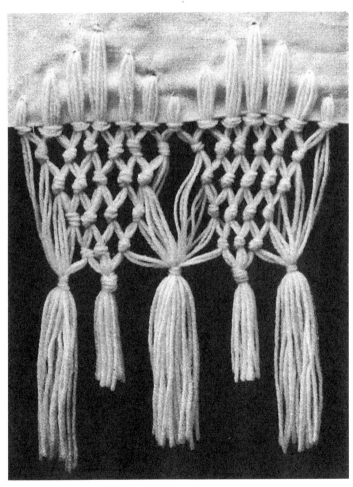

A VANDYKE FRINGE.

5

way of the thread (if twined originally) each half separately, then bring the 2 halves round and round each other in the opposite direction to that in which they were first twined, holding each 'twine' in place the whole time by just changing hands continually; then secure the twine with a knot. When the pattern of the fringe is completed the edges should be evenly trimmed.

MAKING THE VANDYKE FRINGE.

FRINGE NO. 3 IN THE MAKING.

Applied Fringe.

A knotted fringe can be applied on a piece of stitchery. Instead of unravelling the woof, a fringe can be added to it, and can be made of wool, silk, macramé-cotton, or whatever material may suit the work. But it must be remembered that since the fringe is meant to represent the warp, it should correspond both in thickness and in colour. If a wool twice as thick as the material is used for the warp, then one should allow 8 threads intervening space for every 4 threads of the fringe, and so on. For applied fringe cut all your strands the same length to begin with—twice as long as you want the fringe previous to knotting it. Mark out the spaces for threading in the fringe. or if a coarse material, such as canvas, count the threads. Now thread both ends of the fringe-strands into the needle and thread that through the material from the wrong side. Catch the loop with your left 1st finger and thread your needle through that. For the subsequent rows see directions above.

The Colour of the Fringe.

This should always be that of the

actual or apparent warp of the material. By the "apparent" warp is meant any stitchery obviously meant to represent part of the warp, such as in various kinds of tapestry where long stitches are employed the way of the warp. Here the same colours can effectively be continued in the fringe. But where stitchery is obviously of the applied kind, it is in better taste to make the fringe entirely of the same colour as the material.

Its Decorative Use.

Wherever the embroidery suggests the craft of the loom, the fringe is absolutely the most stylish finish, for the very character of the stitchery not only seems incomplete without it, but it positively calls for it as a softening, graceful accompaniment. Consequently, wherever any kind of tapestry, any of the Indian embroideries, or such richly-coloured, tapestry-looking needlecrafts are of decorative effect, that effect is added by a nicely-patterned and carefully-worked fringe.

No. 1. A Twined Fringe.

Of the three fringes illustrated No. 1 is made as follows:—

Measure out equal spaces and cut strands for fringe as directed. This particular fringe takes up a good deal of wool on account of so many twined rows, the original length of strands being 28 inches for a 7-inch fringe.

Double thread through material and knot as directed.

1st Row.—This is twined; the 2nd movement of the twining is repeated 5 times and then the knot is tied.

2nd Row.—Divide the tassels and join the 2 neighbouring halves with a knot.

3rd Row.—As 1st row.
4th Row.—As 2nd row.
5th Row.—As 1st and 3rd rows.
6th Row.—As 2nd and 4th rows.

No. 2. A Vandyke Fringe.

For this Vandyke fringe measure the article to be finished off with fringe and subdivide into spaces of 3 to 4 inches. In each space measure off and mark 1 ascending row and 1 descending one, 4 deep as illustration. If the material is unyielding, the holes should be pierced before threading the fringe through. Then thread as directed.

1st Row.—Knot the fringe, including one-half of the lowest tassel, as only half of this belongs to each motif. The outer half of the initial tassel is thus left free. An illustration shows this in the making. In each of the following rows the outer half of each end-tassel is likewise left free until in the 5th row only one complete tassel with half a tassel on each side is left. These are joined into 1 by a knot.

It is the better plan to do all the "Vandykes" first. The half tassel left free in the last "Vandyke" will, of course, be part of the next motif. When all the Vandykes are completed thread a darning- or crewel-needle with the same kind of wool (or silk) as you are using for the fringe. Gather up the 4 half-tassels on each side into 1 tassel and wind the wool in your needle through that. Secure this "imitation-knot" with a couple of stitches at the back as invisibly as it can possibly be done. All this unknotted work will be found to be considerably longer, and the tassels formed by gathering it up should be trimmed separately and comparatively

The Making of Fringes.

long. Then trim the short tassels on the Vandyke movements.

No. 3. An Easily-made Fringe.

For this quickly-made and effective pattern measure out 2-inch spaces. Measure and mark an independent and detached "movement" in each space as illustrated. This fringe looks best when worked with 4 strands to every stitch. Thread through from the right side all the 5 holes of each "movement," then gather up all the loops in your left hand and all the ends (on the wrong side of the material) in your right hand. Thread all the ends through the united group of loops. An illustration shows this fringe in the making, the silk being tied round the united group of loops to be held by the left hand. Pinning to a cushion or securing by weights laid on is, of course, necessary. Arrange nicely the pattern thus formed. Make a knot.

The 2nd and 3rd rows are knotted ones.

A STAR D'OILY IN HUNGARIAN EMBROIDERY.   Directions for this work appear on page 1.

A Lesson in Netting

No kind of lace combines the qualities of elegance, durability and general usefulness so much as filet lace. It is most decorative, whether on household linen, such as tea-cloths, bedspreads, tray-cloths, and a quantity of other things, or as trimmings on

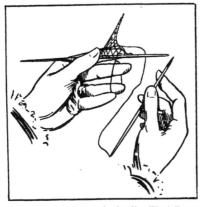

Hands in position ready for the First Loop.

muslin or Shantung silk dresses. Cushion-covers and curtains are made both attractive and valuable when composed of netting inlets in conjunction with Broderie Anglaise, Italian or French embroidery, and various kinds of pillow lace. Filet lace lasts a life-time—and more—if carefully washed. And, lastly, it is a most fascinating handicraft.

We have become accustomed to consider the art of making filet lace as having originated in the Italian convents. But though the nuns made netting into a high art of lace-making, and as such handed it down to us, they themselves most probably got

the idea from the Orient, where embroidery on netted silk-foundation with gold and silver thread, and all the rich colours of the Orient, was one of the common forms of applied art in the early centuries. Where the idea first sprang from to make the common fishing-net mesh out of linen and silk, and to employ it for ornamental purposes, is not known. Still less do we know how, when or where the fishing nets themselves were invented.

Materials Required.

The implements required for making filet lace are a netting-needle, generally made of steel, a flat ivory mesh, and a piece of twine about 1½ yards long. The material is linen-thread. (Barbour's 3-Cord Linen Lace Thread.) If a heavy cushion is available, the twine will not be required. A coarse piece of thread half a yard

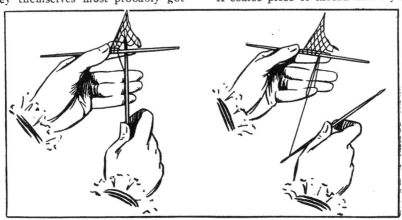

Bobbin passed behind Mesh through Loop.   Ready to draw up the Knot.

A Lesson in Netting.

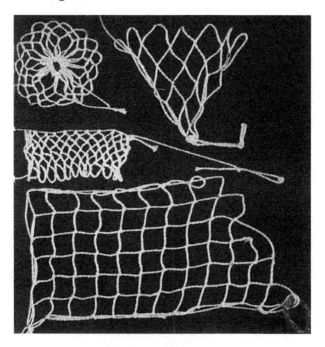

The two top designs show respectively a Star and a piece of Square Netting. Just below is a sample of Oblique Netting, and the bottom design is an oblong piece in the making.

cut from the ball and tied securely to the foundation-loop.

Making the Knot.

Hold the mesh with your right hand, tightening both the thread and the foundation loop. Grasp the mesh with your left hand and you hold it just as you hold your pen with the right hand for writing. Thus holding the mesh, with palm of the hand towards you, bring it beneath the thread to meet the knot that joins the thread and the foundation-loop. Then bring the thread with your right hand tightly round the mesh—the 1st, 2nd and 3rd fingers of left hand. (The needle is held between the thumb and the first and second fingers of right hand.) Bring the thread back between first and second fingers of left hand and in under the thumb, which should hold it securely in place on the mesh, first loop. Then lay the thread in a large semicircle across the foundation-loop and behind your right hand. Holding the needle by the one end, thread the other (upper) end from the left through the first loop, underneath the mesh but above the three fingers of left hand, through the foundation-loop (from underneath upwards). The upper point of the needle should finally rest on the large semicircle where that crosses the foundation-loop. Let go the lower point of the needle and

or less and a pin will do for making the foundation-loop on which to commence the work and hold the netting steady whilst working. If no heavy cushion is at hand, then make a loop of your twine, put your left foot through it and let the heel prevent it from slipping off.

The beginner should begin on some coarser material such as "Bright-eye" or "Peri-lusta," and a mesh at least a quarter of an inch wide. The needle is forked at both ends and has generally an "eye" at the one end. Thread the needle and tie a knot to secure, then run the thread along both sides of the needle and through the forks until twice the thickness of the flat ivory-mesh you mean to use. (The beginner should use a flat mesh, as the round ones are not so easy to keep in place.) The thread should now be

10

grasp the upper one, draw the thread through, catch the loop (second loop) with your fourth finger, then release the thread from between the thumb and the mesh, retract second and third fingers from 1st loop, while tightening it with the right hand. When the 1st loop is quite tightened round the mesh only, the fourth finger should be withdrawn from the 2nd loop; tightening the thread with your right hand will secure

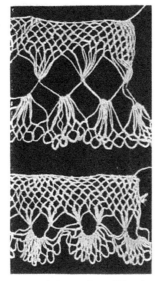

Two Edgings netted obliquely.

the knot. It is important that the mesh should be held in place the whole time just beneath the connecting knot and at a right angle with the foundation-loop. Also never let the little finger release its hold on the 2nd loop until the second and third fingers have released their hold on the 1st loop and that loop is tightened round the mesh. Otherwise the netting will be uneven. The illustrations show the correct positions.

Oblique Netting.

The beginner should practise on an "oblique" piece of netting. Make a row of, say, 20 loops on a foundation-loop, which should be about 4 to 6 inches long, looped at both ends and pinned at either end on to a heavy cushion. Then draw

the mesh out, unpin, and turn your foundation-loop, bring the mesh just to meet the row of loops and make your 2nd row each loop to the one just above it, always working from the left to the right, unpin, draw the mesh out again, and so on. The knack of making an even mesh is easily acquired in half to one hour.

Many pretty edgings for tray-cloths, etc., can be made on the oblique by using different sizes of mesh, joining 2 or more loops of the last row with 1 loop of the row in making, or *vice versâ*. By adding separately-made wheels we come very near the Armenian lace, which is also

A D'oily showing different sizes of mesh.

made by loops and knots. The elaborateness of the design depends, of course, on the ingenuity and proficiency of the worker. A netted d'oily-edging is also an oblique netting. The foundation-loop should be round, and it should be turned to the left continually; instead of working backwards and forwards as in a piece of obliquely-netted lace, the foundation-loop should be tightened into the required circumference as soon as the 1st row of loops is made, the last loop thus being made to meet the 1st one. Then the netting is done round and round. The more variety in the size of mesh and the greater amount of "fans," contrived

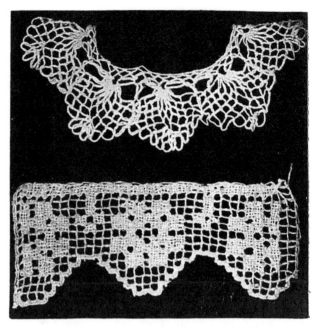

A Netted Edging and a Darned Net Edging.

by means of joining several loops of the previous row into one knot, or branching off a number of loops from one single loop of the previous row, the prettier will the general effect be.

Netting a Square Foundation for Embroidery.

This should be done over a very fine mesh; a flat bone one. one-eighth of an inch, is easier to manipulate, otherwise a fine knitting needle will serve the purpose. Begin by making 2 loops into the foundation-loop, turn, then make 2 loops in the last loop of every row, thus increasing by 1 loop until the requisite width is attained. It will be seen that all netting is done obliquely, a square being commenced at one of the corners. Also that the outsides of the netting is everywhere strengthened by an additional loop. Thus one should always count 2 loops extra.

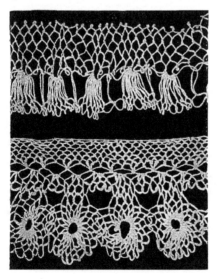

The Lower Edging has separately netted wheels.

Now when you have the 2 loops more than the desired width, 1 row should be netted without increasing. Then join the last 2 loops of every row, thus decreasing the number of loops by 1. When, at last, there are only 2 loops left, the mesh should be withdrawn before the final knot is secured. If the increasing, the straight row, and the decreasing have been done as directed, the finished piece of netting when stretched out is the straight square ready for embroidery.

Oblong Pieces of Netting.

Begin as for square netting. When the width is attained, and 1 row is netted without increasing, increase every other row and decrease every other (begin by increasing.) When the length is reached, decrease as for the square piece.

Knots.

Except when the thread breaks accidentally, all the knots should be at the edge. When the thread on the needle is not long enough to last the next row through, it should be cut off to within an inch; the needle should be refilled, and the new thread joined on by means of a sailor knot (never a "granny-knot"!) quite close to the last knot made by the netting. Knots within the netted square itself are very ugly and should be avoided.

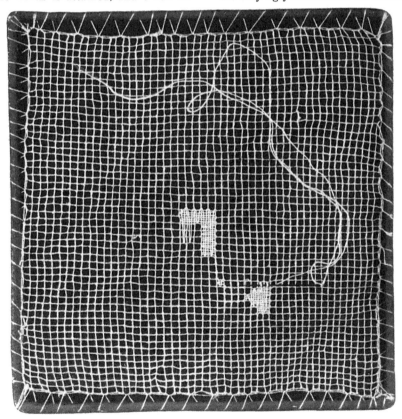

Net being darned in a frame.

A Lesson in Netting.

Embroidering on the Net.

The net should be tacked into a wire-frame, each corner first firmly secured in place, then the sides opposite each other, two at the time, so that the net is evenly stretched.

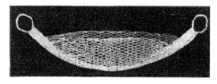

A Hammock in Miniature.

The stitch mostly used is the darning-stitch, *point toile*. When consisting of only 2 threads in the warp and 2 in the weft, the lace is called "Filet Antique." Do as much of the warp as can be done of the pattern before beginning the weft. Only one "fastening" is allowed, the new thread being joined to the old one by a sailor-knot. When beginning at a new spot follow round the edges of the darning, twining or "over-sewing" round the thread of the netting, when that can be followed ; if not, take the nearest way to the point where darning should recommence in the same manner.

The same kind of thread can be used for darning filet lace as for netting the foundation, or Barbour's Irish Silk Floss Embroidery Thread.

About Meshes.

For the sake of clearness, the word "mesh" has only been used for the implement so-called. The netting is often called mesh, and so are the loops. An even piece of netting is, for instance, called "even mesh," and a certain number of loops is termed so many "meshes." This is quite correct, but somewhat bewildering in a set of directions.

The worker will sometimes find that the meshes are not always true, but very often a lead-pencil or a coarse steel knitting-needle will give a more perfect circle (when a round mesh is used). This, however, the worker will soon find out for herself.

How to Make a Hammock.

Some girls may want to start something really useful and will like to attempt a hammock. Any strong kind of twine should be used for this, and a very big netting-needle. The hammock is netted obliquely, 40 loops in every row throughout the entire length of the hammock.

The foundation-loop should go over the foot, as the material is too heavy for pinning the work on to a weighted cushion. For netting the 1st and 2nd rows, a thin but strongly-bound book should be used as mesh. Then 35 to 40 rows (according to the length desired) are netted over a wooden mesh 1½ inches wide, and the last 2 rows are again netted across the same book as was used for the first 2 rows.

The foundation-loop should be moved from time to time as the work grows, threading it through every mesh of the last but one completed row. This should be repeated whenever the work has grown to such a length as to be uncomfortably near the worker's face. When the netting of the hammock is complete, the final knot should be strengthened by an additional knot. The mesh should be withdrawn from the loop before securing this knot.

Now gather up all the loops of the last row in your left hand, run the twine 6 times through and join all six rings thus formed into one, either by crocheting or buttonholing (also with the twine). This makes an extra strong ring to fasten the hammock on to a tree. A similar ring should be made by taking up the loops of the 1st row. It will be found that they are "looped" at the end as they were netted on to the already with-drawn foundation-loop. These little knots are easily undone by stretching each loop separately. The end of twine at the very beginning of the netting should also be secured. And the two strong rings for the cord should be exactly alike at either end.

Dress Trimming in Rhodes Embroidery or Punched Work.

Collars and Cuffs would look effective in this style of work.

Beautiful trimmings for dresses made of some material of an open texture can very easily be made in this popular style of fancy work. Any geometrical design can be traced on the fabric, such as that illustrated here, then the outside edge is worked over with overcasting stitch; the openwork section is done on the counted threads. Commencing at the first 3 threads inside the line at the left side, with fine linen thread and a very coarse tapestry needle, insert the needle between the 3rd and 4th threads in the fabric, from the top, catch the end of the thread as it follows the needle, bring the latter up before the 1st thread in a horizontal line, then pass it down through the 1st hole again, crossing the end of the thread to secure it, bring it up through the 2nd hole and down through the 1st again, * pass the needle diagonally on the back and bring it up through the 3rd and 4th threads in a perpendicular line below the 2nd hole, insert between the 3rd and 4th threads in a horizontal

An Effective Dress Trimming.

line with the last hole, and bring it up again through the preceding hole, then down through the hole to the right, * repeat to the end of the 1st perpendicular line of openwork in the design, turn the work upside down and repeat over next 3 threads and continue in this way until all the perpendicular lines are worked, then turn the work the other way and work the horizontal lines in exactly the same manner. The lower edge is worked in buttonhole stitch with coarse embroidery cotton and the centre flower with the same kind of thread. Make a hole in the very centre of the motif with the coarse needle, then work a row of buttonhole stitch around it, using, of course, an ordinary embroidery needle for the purpose. The petals are worked thus: After finishing the centre hole put a stitch on the edge of the first one or two stitches to get the thread exactly opposite the centre of one of the little squares that surround this centre, stretch the thread along the centre and make a stitch in about the

The Berlin Wool-work Designs on this page are described in the next article.

Suitable for a Cushion: Background dark brown, Cross-bars gold, Centre Design cream.

Variety can often be obtained by combining one or two Simple Motifs.

4th thread from the edge, insert the needle in the edge of the buttonhole stitch through which it comes out and stretch another thread to the top stitch where you run the needle under the same thread in the fabric; this gives 3 threads over which you work darning stitch from side to side, taking alternately two and one of the threads on the needle down to the centre, where you pass the stitch through the buttonhole stitches until exactly opposite the centre of next square, where you repeat the petal, and so on all round for the 8 petals. The material is next cut away from the outside of the buttonhole edging.

Collars, revers, and cuffs in this pattern will give a very dainty finish to the costume made of linen, and of course, may be, with advantage, worked on a coarser material of a contrasting colour, or white: Hardanger canvas is a very suitable material for the white or ecru work, and so are the new shirting canvasses of mercerised cotton.

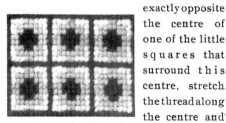

A Neat Design for Waistbelt, in three colours to harmonise with the Gown.

Rose pink, pale green and white would combine well for the above Design.

Berlin Wool=work.

The revival of the mid-Victorian Berlin wool-work is a useful one. Like every form of needlecraft, it has been abused, and always will be abused if it gets into the hands of the inartistic worker, who has neither good judgment—nor a good pattern—to guide her. But when treated artisti-

Suitable for Inlets for a Cushion.

tional. As a matter of fact, its very convention-ality is an advan-tage in many instances, because a worker who has the sense to know when her powers are only very limited can get a good motif, and repeat it with excellent effect, without any demand on artistic percep-

These Bells would look pretty for a Fancy Work Bag.

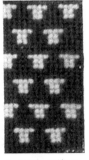

A simple pattern for a Fancy Waistcoat.

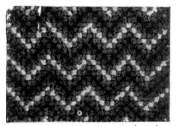

Waved lines in various shades of the same colour are effective.

cally, and used in the right place, this work has very desirable qualities, and is to be preferred to many of the looser, coarse forms of embroid-ery, even though it may be much more conven-

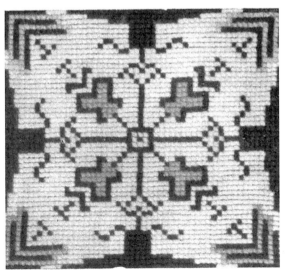

A Bold Design in three colours for a Cushion Centre or a Footstool.

tion, or clever workman-ship — which may be beyond her.

The good wearing quality of this work is undeni-able; the canvas gives a staying power to the whole, and the

Berlin Wool Work.

A Design in black, violet, heliotrope and white. Could be used in various ways.

thickness of the crossed wool or thread makes a thoroughly strong firm substance when completed.

I saw a most interesting example of the durability of this work in the home of the late Mrs. Emma Brewer, whose name was so well known to the older readers of *The Girl's Own Paper.*

The long corridors in her flat were carpeted with lengths of this work, most exquisitely worked, in a conventional pattern in which dark tones predominated, but were relieved with

If you thought of trying a Mat, this Design would look very well.

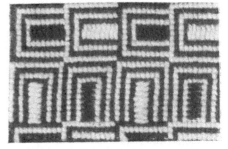

A quiet device that could be used as a Belt, a Cushion, or a Teapot Mat.

brighter touches of colour. The work was the width of moderately wide stair carpet, and in lengths each several yards long. When I remarked on the beauty of the work, and exclaimed against such handiwork being walked upon, Mrs. Brewer smiled in her way—which was a very charming way—and said, "But, my dear child, it may just as well be serving a useful purpose, and where

it can be seen, as be rolled up and put away to make a happy hunting ground for moth!" And then she told me how, in her early married life, when her husband—a Member of Parlia-

Bands of trimming like the three-colour blocks above would look well at the edge of plain Winter Curtains, such as serge or rep.

ment—was often late at the House, she used to fill up the time by doing this work while waiting up for him. In those Victorian days the gentlewomen did great things in the way of needlework, and there is every indication that the reign of Queen Mary will show some equally fine records.

But though everyone may not have the courage to attempt such large pieces of work as these strips done by Mrs. Brewer, there are scores of less ambitious ways in which the work can be used to great advantage. Only remember this: its great beauty lies

A Crazy Pattern that will amuse children.

in a right selection of colour. And here the modern worker has an immense advantage

Above is a Design that would look well for Belts, or for trimming Children's Winter Frocks.

over the earlier workers. Silks and wools are now obtainable in a variety of delicate and beautiful shades that would have fairly dazzled our ancestresses. Baldwin's Beehive Fingering can be had in a number of beautiful colours, and is very suitable. And to these must be added the wonderful range now available in the mercerised cottons, and the various pretty glossy threads, such as Peri-Lusta, that modern ingenuity has produced from wood fibre! All these wear well, and though the cotton threads may not be quite

Carried out in apple-green diamonds, outlined with black, and completed with white.

as lasting as the wools, they do well for things that are not required to live indefinitely, and are only wanted for a time.

It is not necessary that men's fancy waistcoats, for instance, or dress trimmings, or girls' waistbelts, should last for a generation. If they serve a couple of seasons, that is usually enough; one is tired of the pattern by then, and craving something new; for these the mercerised threads are usually all that can be desired. On the other hand, for cushions, bags,

fancy strips for chairs and such-like upholstery, where the work will be acceptable, and delightful, and useful for as long as ever it can be made to last, a good quality wool, with dyes guaranteed to fade as little as possible will be the best to use, and the beauty of this will be greatly enhanced if a

This would look well in Bands as a dress-trimming for serge or cloth.

stout rope silk, or Esplen D'or, is introduced in touches. It will brighten the work and give it richness and character.

As a general rule, this work looks best when it consists of a repeated simple conventional design. Now and again one comes on sprays of flowers, birds, and such-like subjects that have been produced with good effect, but these are exceptional: more often they look crude and angular; whereas a small recurring pattern has charm of its own in its very simplicity and monotony. One point about this work will especially commend

The Design above is most suited to a Fancy Bag. This work looks well if used for the lower half of the Bag, the upper half being of silk.

it to the girl with small pocket money, and that is the cheapness of the material as compared with work done on linen or any other material that is to show when the work is finished.

Pincushions in Cut Work.

A Crescent-shaped Pincushion.

To make this pretty pincushion, commence by following with a fine needle the line on one side of the figure with small casting sts. Then work down the other side until you come to where the first bar is to be placed. Take a st across, making a bar between the two lines (see Fig, 1). Now 1 st back. Fasten these sts firmly. Take 1 more st across and fasten in the opposite side. You have now a bar of 3 threads. Turn your needle, and holding the point between your finger and thumb, work with the blunt end over and over the threads

A CRESCENT-SHAPED PINCUSHION.

A RETICELLA PINCUSHION.

of the bar until, with close, even sts, you reach the opposite side. Turn your needle again and continue basting around until the next bar is reached, when the process is repeated.

When the bars are finished, cut the material away beneath, being careful not to cut the bars. Free the bars with your needle, and work all round the design with the simple over and over binding st.

The back of the pincushion may be embroidered the same as the front, or left plain, but both edges are scalloped and button-holed, and eyelet holes worked near the edge,

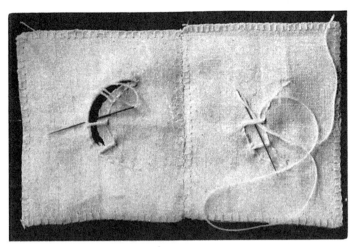

Fig. 1. MAKING THE BARS AND CUTTING AWAY THE MATERIAL.

and button-
hole round,
with the
purl sts on
the outside.

Then make
a 2nd row of
loose button-
hole sts in
every 2nd st,
after which
take 1 bind-
ing st in
each of those
loose loops to
make them
firmer and

through which ribbon is run. The
pincushion is finished with a bow on
each end, allowing a good length for
hanging it. Worked entirely in
white and laid over pink, with pink
ribbons, the effect is very beautiful.

A Reticella Pincushion.

The square pincushion is rather
more difficult than the other, but
even here, the great essential is care,
and if the
work is fol-
lowed step
by step, as
shown in
the working
directions
(Fig. 2), even
this will be
found to be
within the
possibilities
of the aver-
age worker.

Start with
the middle
figure.
Pierce a hole
in the centre

stronger.

The 3rd row consists of a series of
triangles, all worked in buttonhole st.
Fill the 1st hole with sts, turn, and
work back on top of them. Take a
2nd row of buttonhole sts on top,
only making this row 2 sts less than
the 1st, work back again. Continue
until there is only 1 st left. Then
take a few overcasting sts down the

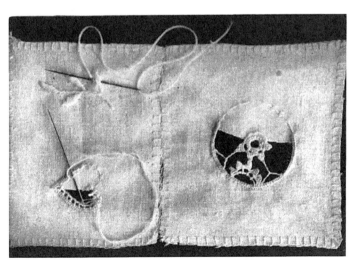

Fig. 2. WORKING THE CENTRAL FIGURE. HEART-SHAPED
FIGURE AND SOLID EMBROIDERY.

side of the triangle, and start the next triangle in the 2nd hole.

Baste round the circle which encloses the central figure. This is also buttonholed round. As the circle is worked, the triangles are connected with the crossing bars, which, as will be seen, are of the thread twisted over and over. As the embroidery is done, the material is carefully cut away on the wrong side.

For the heart-shaped figures, first take small basting sts round, then a row of close buttonhole stitching, and on top of that a row of loose buttonholing. A few sts are then carried across to fill the figure in.

Make the upper and under side of the pincushion cover of the same size, and hemstitch each to the depth of an inch. Then lace with cord.

AN ACORN DESIGN IN DARNED FILET NET.

Filet Lace Squares.

A DESIGN SHOWING SIMPLE OUTLINES.

Filet brodé or darned net, n o w coming so much to the front, is a most fascinating form of fancy-work, and not so difficult as it may seem to the inexperienced worker. The point to be most particular about is to see that the right thread is used, as this makes a great difference to the work.

The first step is the netted background—this is made in the ordinary way with a mesh, according to size desired. For this part of the work use Barbour's 3-cord Linen L a c e Thread.

The square or strip thus obtained, is then stretched on a wire frame (these frames are to be obtained in any large needlework department).

The design is now carried out in "point de toile" or darning stitch, with a rather blunt needle, and thread (the thread should be a little finer than the mesh). Barbour's Irish Silk Floss Embroidery Thread is suitable for this.

After tying thread to the mesh with the needle, pass alternately over and under a thread of the mesh,

AN EFFECTIVE PATTERN.

according to design ; an effort should be made to connect the design as far as possible, thus avoiding o p e n spaces. Continue to fill in the holes with two or three threads, now work over and under these threads crosswise, giving darned effect.

The work is more easily accomplished by beginning at the corner of a design—but great care must be taken in counting the number of holes, etc., as a mistake is so easily made. Knots must be avoided ; when taking a new thread attach to last with a very small knot which becomes invisible in the darning.

The squares illustrated are most effective for inserting in table-linen, etc. The same design worked in a finer make of mesh and thread make a very elaborate finish to a frock or blouse.

Catalan Embroidery.

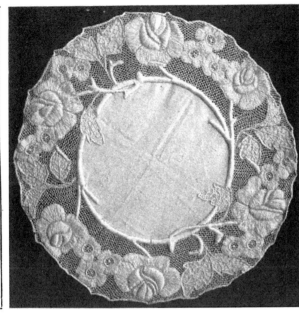

A Handsome Centrepiece in Catalan Embroidery.

An enlarged section appears on another page.

The Centrepiece.

The drawing should be traced upon a large square of linen or oatmeal cloth. (Pencil marks will soil the threads). Fix the material very firmly into an embroidery frame. Cover the whole with fine butter-muslin or white paper. Cut a door and pin back whilst working. This method keeps the work from becoming soiled.

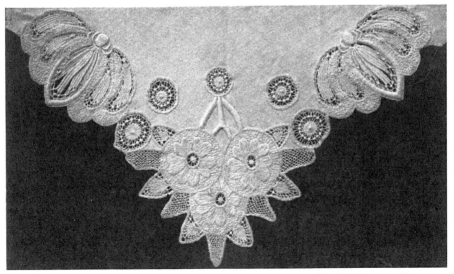

A TEA CLOTH BORDER.

The directions are the same as for the Butterfly.

Catalan Embroidery.

Use Coton Perlé "Lustrous" D.M.C., No. 8.

Begin with the "mesh" or net-stitch. This is very simple work, merely tiny loops worked evenly back and forth. Work this "mesh" in and out between the drawing, taking care that each side is sewn well within the flower, leaf, and outer edges, otherwise the stitches may break away when the material is cut out underneath.

with snow knots. To make the snow knots use double thread and leave tiny, even loops upon the upper surface of material. After the leaves are embroidered fill in the bare spaces with these snow knots or very small cross-stitch. Finish off all outer edges of flowers and leaves with a firm buttonhole stitch.

The trunk and all narrow sprays are merely smooth satin stitches.

When all is finished, remove from

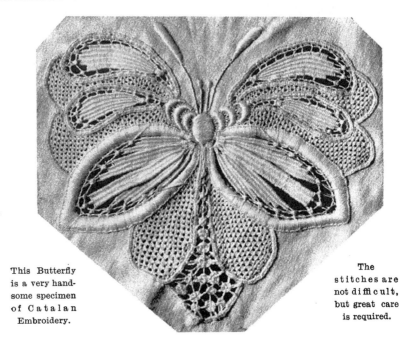

This Butterfly is a very handsome specimen of Catalan Embroidery.

The stitches are not difficult, but great care is required.

Now commence work upon the rose by making tiny cross or back stitches between each petal. Pad these petals with any kind of soft, white thread. Carefully embroider each portion of the flower and finish off with a narrow buttonhole stitch all around the outside. This will hold flower and mesh firmly together.

In the smaller flowers there is no padding. The centres can be cut out for tiny openwork, or filled in

frame and work a narrow buttonhole edging all around the outside of the embroidery. Turn over, cut away the material from under the mesh, also from the buttonhole edging.

The insertions illustrated are worked in the same way.

The Butterfly.

A square of coarse linen or oatmeal cloth is needed.

The design should first be drawn upon paper. If drawn upon the

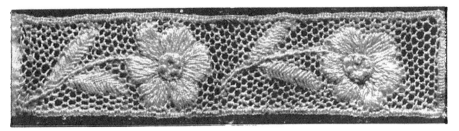

A NARROW INSERTION.

material great care must be taken, otherwise the pencil marks will soil the threads. Commence by running a single thread aroun1 all the drawing. Use Ardern's new "Lustrous" Thread. Work a tight, but narrow, buttonhole stitch around the upper parts of wing and lower parts of body and tail.

Now fix material very tightly in an embroidery frame. Work head and the half-hoops with a firm satin-stitch. Between these hoops and between the buttonhole work of wings sew tiny stitches, drawing the linen threads apart, as in Rhodes Embroidery.

Upper Wings.

Cut away the unworked material from the upper parts of wings close to the buttonhole work, making 2 holes on both sides of the open-worked parts.

Around each of these holes make from 10 to 14 loop stitches. Don't draw them too tightly, or the work will pucker when washed. Now return to the top of the hole and work upon it a small ring of 3 threads. Into this ring cast on 6 long threads, passing each thread through a small loop at the bottom of hole. At the top of these 6 threads make a small tassel-knot. Take a needleful of very long thread. Sew it firmly into this tassel-knot. Take 2 of the 6 long threads and darn them closely back and forth until nearly at the bottom

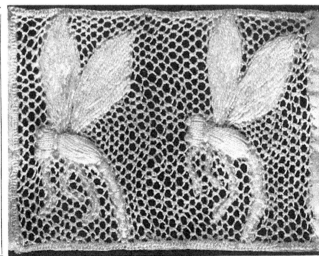

A Design composed of Satin Stitch and Net Stitch.

This would make a good pattern for a beginner.

of the hole. Pass the needle here and there through one of the tiny side loops, fastening each firmly. Continue darning until at the bottom, first around the lower threads and finish with fancy knot. When 2 of the 6 threads have been darned on both sides, return to the 2 long threads in the middle, darn in the same manner, but continue until almost at the bottom of hole, thus forming the point. Finish with fancy knot.

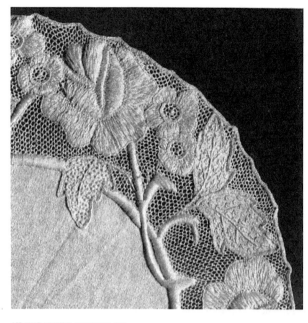

AN ENLARGED SECTION OF THE CENTREPIECE.

Lower Left and Right Wings.

Begin the outer edge, and near the head, with a narrow buttonhole stitch, gradually making it much wider towards the bottom. Care must be taken that the sides are even.

Cut out material and make 19 small stitches upon the sides of the hole, commencing in the middle. This done, return to top of hole and work 4 threads across for a ring, buttonhole it and cast on 19 long threads. Pass each thread into a loop at the side

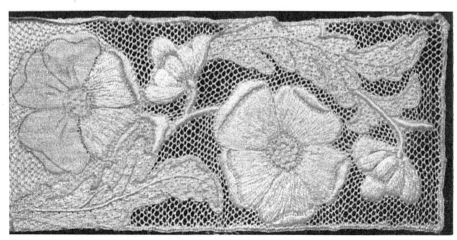

THIS INSERTION IS WORKED IN THE SAME MANNER AS THE CENTREPIECE.

of hole and continue until each is finished. Return to top and button-hole very firmly twice across the 19 threads, close to ring. Split these threads into groups of 4, on either side, leaving 3 for the middle. Darn down the 4 threads, in the same manner as in the upper wing, as far as the 1st loop at the sides. Finish off each with fancy knots. The 3 long middle threads must be darned until nearly at the bottom of hole and finish with knots.

Around the body work a very narrow and firm buttonhole stitch, and fill in with Rhodes Embroidery (or Punched Work). The tail is filled in with woven wheels.

The tea-cloth corner is worked in the same manner as the butterfly.

A CUSHION COVER IN BARO EMBROIDERY.   For directions see next page.

The New Baro Embroidery.

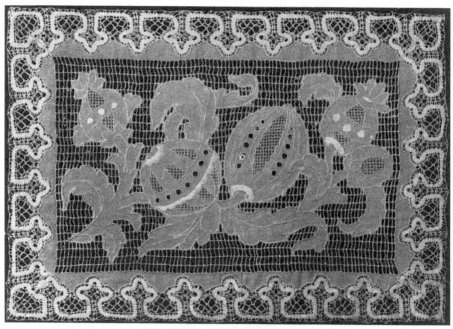

A Handsome copyright Design, by the
Broderie Russe Co.

It really seems nowadays as if needle-work and embroidery were made so simple that most effective results can be produced with a minimum of trouble and difficulty. In the new Baro work, of which some exquisite samples are illustrated on these pages, there is no drawing of threads that is so trying to the eyes. All that are required are a little care and patience, and the work is quite within the possibilities of anyone who can do buttonhole stitch and binding stitch, which is simply an over and over stitch.

Materials Required.

The materials required are few and simple. First there is the design, which can be bought ready traced on to the material for d'oilies, tea-cloths, cushion-covers, or practically any-thing else. Then a sharp pair of embroidery scissors will be required, a crewel needle, and some Baro embroidery thread.

How the Work is Done.

The first thing to do is to buttonhole stitch the design all round (binding stitch may be used for this part of the work if preferred, but buttonholing is the most general). This must be done before any of the cutting is com-menced, or the material will fray and be spoilt. Now take the scissors and snip along the lines marked in the diagram A A to B B. Around the little bar thus formed, sew firmly over and over in simple binding stitch. keeping the point of the needle in the hand and working with the other end, as this is so much easier. When this bar is finished, cut on the adjoining lines C D, and work in the same way. Con-tinue to work in this way over the

30

cloth. It is really best to snip the bars for the width of the work first, as it is then possible to continue sewing over and over without stopping to cut in between. When the other side of the cloth is reached,

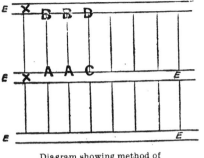

Diagram showing method of working.

snip down the next set of lines and work back again in the same way.

Over the vertical bars E (which are formed by the previous stitches, and do not need to be cut), the same over and over stitch is worked, and a cross-stitch is made where the horizontal and vertical bars intersect one another.

Any further embroidery stitches can

now be added to the solid part of the design, and a most suitable finish to this handsome work is an edge of Cluny lace.

As will be seen from the samples of work we illustrate, the background mesh can be varied, some being squares, some more oblong, etc. A clever worker soon gets to make many varieties.

Where to Get the Requisites.

This work is suitable for various purposes, and looks very beautiful when made into curtains or bedspreads. But the worker who does

A finished piece of work, from a copyright design by the Broderie Russe Co.

The New Baro Embroidery.

not want to attempt so much at the start may be glad to know that it is equally effective made up into smaller articles, and designs can be purchased traced for d'oilies

Starting a piece of work.

Baro embroidery strengthens the fabric, and gives it an added lease of life, since every thread in the background is gone over again with the embroidery thread.

and tray-cloths, nightdress cases, etc. These designs and all requisites for the embroidery can be obtained from the Broderie Russe Co., 289, Regent Street, London, W.

One of the admirable qualities of this work is its durability. Whereas drawn threads often weaken the fabric, no matter how beautiful the design,

The interesting variation in the background of the cushion cover design on page 29 is given by catching two bars together in the middle. Notice too, in this handsome piece of work, the various methods that have been employed for filling in the leaves, hardly any two being alike.

An effective little square made by darning filet crochet.

Innishmacsaint Lace.

When Queen Alexandra last visited Ireland, the women of that country, who always had a respectful liking for her, were puzzling over what offering they could make that would express in any suitable manner their regard and esteem, and at the same time be acceptable, they thought of this Innishmacsaint lace, and unanimously agreed upon it. It is the most precious of all the Irish laces, and is very like the rare old Venetian Point. A length of this was made and tied around a bouquet of choice flowers, which was presented to Her Majesty. It is said that she appreciated the beauty of the offering very much, as well as the manner in which it was made.

The lace is made in the finest of linen thread in the natural colour, and though so very fine is not at all difficult to make, as the stitches used are only variations of the well-known buttonhole stitch, but the very fine stitchery required is somewhat trying to the eyes if the worker be not blessed with very keen sight; therefore only a small piece should be worked at a time, and there is no reason why anyone who can sew very neatly should not make a few motifs in this charming lace, if only for the purpose of learning how to make it. An idea of the costliness of this needle point may be formed from the fact that lace, only 3 inches deep, will cost from 52/- a yard upwards when of the best quality.

The piece of lace illustrated was worked with No. 100 Irish Lace Thread, linen, in the natural colour, that is unbleached, a very coarse soft linen thread was employed for the "high relief" edges and rings, a very particular feature of this class of lace. The first thing to do is to prepare the design, but these can be had already made from the fancy-work depôts. They are usually composed of the design traced on green linen or glazed calico in heavy black lines, and these are best, as the green background makes the stitching less trying and more distinct. If from any reason one of these is not obtainable then the design must be drawn on a piece of paper and transferred to the glazed calico, or it can be worked on a small piece of tough paper if only a single motif be required.

Tack the paper securely to a piece

Innishmacsaint Lace.

of coarse linen, then take 5 or 6 strands of the linen thread and fold them into a cord long enough to cover the outlines of the design. Beginning at the end of a stem or leaf, lay this cord along the outline and fasten over it with a st across the cord, bring the needle up from underneath beside the cord somewhat less than ⅛-inch from the last st, insert the needle from the other side of the cord through the same hole and pull the thread, not too tightly, but so as to keep the outlining even, then repeat this st until the entire outline has been covered. All the lines, including the little rings, must be outlined with this cord. You then

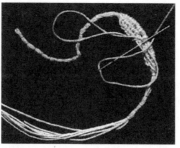

WORKING THE LACE STITCH.

proceed to fill in the centres with the various kinds of buttonhole st, taking great care to keep the work as clean as possible. For this purpose only the part in actual use should be left uncovered; the other portion should have a piece of white paper tacked over it, and if the strip be long it must be folded and pinned into a

roll, then on the working portion the fingers should touch it as little as possible; a scrap of tissue paper wound round the thumb of the left hand and tightly twisted at the top to keep it secure is the readiest way to prevent soiling from that useful member which is the finger that comes most often into contact with it. The sts must always end at a traced line; there can be no joining in the centre or any other part, and when the thread gets too short it must be run 2 or 3 times into the tracing line to secure it, without making the tracing too thick; then cut away, join a new thread by fastening to the outline with a couple of tight sts. A hint of great use to a worker is to always work with the point of the needle turned *from* the worker; the sts are more uniform when this method is adopted.

When all the spaces are filled, the edges, except those in "high relief," are worked over in a close buttonhole st, with the picots if

AN OUTLINE OF THE PATTERN.

necessary. In the sample illustrated there are no picots on the thin buttonholed edges, but they are plentiful on those in relief. For the edges in high relief, you take a very coarse linen thread of the same colour, or fold the outlining cord in three as a substitute, and work the buttonhole sts over this into the edge of the leaf. The large rings are also worked over this thick padding and the little loops with picots formed while working the buttonhole sts. It will be more convenient to work the small rings separately, and then sew them in place.

To Work the Buttonhole Stitch.

Commence at the right side of a line and work a row evenly and closely to the opposite side, make a st into the outlining cord and bring the thread back across the top of the sts to the point where you began the row, make a st into the outlining cord here, then work back over this thread into the sts of the 1st row, taking care to go into every st, and where there is a diamond, stripe, or other figure in little openwork holes, you pass over 2 or 3 sts by stretching the thread across the thread already there and even with it, then when coming back work the same number of sts over the 2 threads as were missed in the previous row.

To make a Picot.

At the point where you require the picot to be you insert a pin through the linen, pass the thread once around this pin to form a tiny upstanding loop, make a st on the edge, then put a couple of sts around the stem of the loop and continue along the edge to the next picot, and so on.

The little loops with picots are made by turning the thread back and forming a loop by making a tight st into the edge about 10 sts to the right : form another loop over this and fasten to the left, then bring the thread back to the right again and fasten into the 1st st, thus getting 3 threads to work over.

The bars that connect the different portions of the design are all worked over a single thread, and there are single or double loops with picots worked on the centre of all the longer bars.

The top edge is worked before the filling of the bars, of course ; the 2 horizontal lines are outlined with the thick thread, then buttonholed and the space between filled with diagonal bars. In the lower edge the horizontal line is also of the coarse thread, and the loops and picots are formed while working the buttonholing over the line.

The lace is removed from the design by cutting the threads on the back of the design.

When the stitchery is finished, place the lace between folds of linen wrung out from hot water, press with a hot iron until the linen is nearly dry, only on the wrong side of the lace. Remove the linen from under the lace, and keep pressing over the upper piece until the lace is quite dry. The front of the lace should show out in high relief and the lace be quite crisp and fresh.

Reticella Lace Squares.

The band round the central figure has the buttonholes spaced.

Here the Picots on the Corded Bars give a light effect.

This work is made with a rather coarse make of linen thread, which gives a heavy, rich effect, and is most suitable for inserting in bed, table linen, etc.

The design should first be traced on moleskine or architect's drawing paper. The principal lines of tracing are now outlined with two strands of the thread, which are couched down at intervals with needle and ordinary sewing cotton. This serves as foundation for the work and is most important.

Buttonhole stitch is chiefly employed for this work. The "brides or barrettes" are made by stretching the thread across space three times, and buttonholing.

The thicker parts of the work,

A Star Pattern. The triangles are composed of spaced buttonholes.

The five central bars crossing in the centre are in Binding Stitch.

principally the small triangles, are worked as follows :—1 row of buttonhole stitch over outline thread, throw thread across from right to left, pass needle under 1st buttonhole stitch, work as before with buttonhole stitch into each stitch of former row and *over* thread.

For the parts where a lighter effect is required the 1st row of buttonhole stitches instead of being close together are slightly spaced ; in the following row a stitch is placed between each, and in the next rows alternately.

In some parts a corded effect is obtained by simply pressing thread closely under outline thread and drawing up tightly.

When the work is completed, the couching stitches are done and the square taken off the paper and firmly pressed on the wrong side with a hot iron.

The Story of Amager Embroidery.

The present time is the R e n a i s s a n c e period of Handicrafts. Never were national home-industries more f u l l y recognised or held in higher honour than they are to-day. Needleworkers of the highest rank are stud-

modern times at their disposal; aided and inspired, too, by the designers o f h i g h standard who have made such a thorough study of the "Art of n a t i o n a l industry," and who have brought their wider experience

The simplicity of the stitches is here shown. The charm of the work lies in the colouring.

iously examining old stitches and deft- ly reproducing them with the improved implements and various materials of

and their highly cultured taste to bear on the s u b j e c t a n d thus brought it to a completion

AN ENLARGED SECTION OF THE CENTREPIECE.

—the goal of its initiators' aim.

Every kind of national industry has its romance, its own record of steady development, and its own distinct characteristics, which account for its charm.

One of the most charming of old national industries recently brought to light and recognition is Amager-work, so called from the island of Amager, just outside the city of Copenhagen. It portrays the products of the traditional occupation of the inhabitants of that island in a quaintly pictorial manner. Their flowers, shrubs, and herbs were their models, as well as the medium through which they obtained their lovely mellow tints. The subtle gradations of shades found in old Amager colours speaks of an inborn æsthetic instinct, and the prodigality in design, in which new juxtapositions of colour are continually occurring, bespeaks a surprising understanding of the inherent relations of colours. The clusters, wreaths, and "patches" of flowers, all copied "full face" and seldom with any stalks, constitute the designs of Amager-work. The endless variety of colours, achieved by means of plant-dyes, and arranged in exquisite effect, are its distinctive charm.

In addition to the technically interesting type of design, exquisite studies in tone and harmony of colours, there is something essentially Dutch in the character of Amager-work (though its revival and present form is entirely due to the Danes). And no wonder! for the Amager colony was imported from Holland. King Christian II. married a Dutch princess in 1515, and it was undoubtedly owing to her influence that he, in the following year, imported some 30 Dutch families

A BEAUTIFUL CENTREPIECE.
From a Copyright Design by Mr. Chr. Permin, of Copenhagen.

on account of the fame of that nation as gardeners and dairy-farmers. He gave them the fertile island of Amager as a settlement, and the tax he levied on them consisted of dairy produce, vegetables, and herbs for the royal household and retinue.

From that day till now has the Amager people's fame as gardeners maintained its supremacy. And it is one of the most picturesque sights of

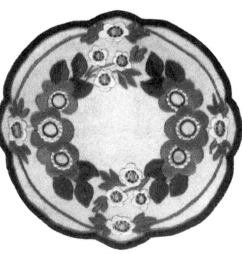

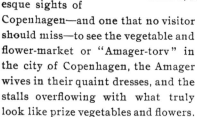

A D'OILY IN SHADES OF RED, BLUE, YELLOW, BLACK AND WHITE.

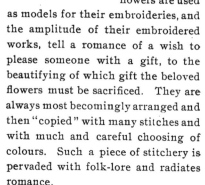

soul of the people. Few national industries appeal, to my mind, more directly to one's emotions than Amager-work. The rich, ripe tints of the thriving cottage-blossoms, arranged in prettily contrasting colours, the bright, plentiful blossoms, tell of cottage-gardens, of love for Nature, and of something more besides. The very mode and manner in which the flowers are used

Copenhagen—and one that no visitor should miss—to see the vegetable and flower-market or "Amager-torv" in the city of Copenhagen, the Amager wives in their quaint dresses, and the stalls overflowing with what truly look like prize vegetables and flowers.

They have preserved their Dutch type, and many of them wear the national dress—maybe somewhat modified since 1516. But they are undoubtedly strong and independent as a clan, though loyal to the core to the adopted land of their forefathers. It was these settlers who initiated the Amager-work.

It has been said that the hall-mark of decorative art, as distinct from merely pleasing ornamentation, is the former's appeal to one's emotions and intellect through the medium of one's senses; and national industries are said to approach the rank and standard of art in proportion as they reveal the

as models for their embroideries, and the amplitude of their embroidered works, tell a romance of a wish to please someone with a gift, to the beautifying of which gift the beloved flowers must be sacrificed. They are always most becomingly arranged and then "copied" with many stitches and with much and careful choosing of colours. Such a piece of stitchery is pervaded with folk-lore and radiates romance.

The modern Amager-work owes its revival and justly-earned reputation to Mr. Chr. Permin, in Copenhagen. He has made a thorough search for authentic models in the shape of Amager aprons, cloths and cushions, etc., and, with his staff of able workers and designers, has not only revived the old industry, but made it to meet modern requirements. And he himself is a past-master in colour-schemes.

The work is most fascinating, and,

40

as the stitch is the same as used in plain embroidery, it is easy. The variety of colours makes it clear for the eyes as well. Everything hinges upon a correctly poised design and the real Amager colours. Last, but not least, Amager-work is most applicable and distinctly decorative.

Hardanger Blouse Trimming.

This pattern can be easily copied as it contains only the simplest of Hardanger stitches. The material used is white Hardanger linen. The outlines and darning are worked in "Bright-eye" weaving, lace stitch and crochet in "Gem Brighteye."

Counting the Threads.

It makes the counting easier to run a piece of cotton over and under 4 threads of the linen for the size required. This also serves as a test of the accuracy of the work; a thread is so easily missed and then the outlines have to be done again.

Darning.

After the outlines of the pattern are finished, run a thread under and over 2 threads across the linen between, miss 2 threads and repeat, starting the thread *over* this time. The satin stitch around is worked over 4 threads.

Lace Stitch.

The lace stitch is done, when the 4 sides are finished, by working a buttonhole stitch into the 4 corners; then overcast each stitch, pulling the thread rather tightly.

Crochet Edge.

Turn the linen in, leaving 2 threads beyond the satin stitch, over this work d c, making the loops long enough to cover the linen edge. 6 d c, 5 ch, sl st back into 4th stitch, into loop work 5 d c, 1 picot, 5 d c.

A Brussels Braid Lace Collar.

This most effective-looking lace is quite simple to make, and the work is very quickly executed. The design shown is from Mr. William Barnard, 126, Edgware Road, London, W., and he is able to supply all the materials.

A fine Brussels net and the two varieties of lace braid shown will be needed to make the collar, also lace thread for filling-in purposes.

First tack the Brussels net over the design, and then place the fancy braid round the edge as shown in the illustration, whipping the inner side of each curve. Arrange the straight braid where required and fasten securely with a tiny hemming stitch. Then fill in the twisted bars where shown.

The small leaves are made by cutting the ovals of the fancy braid apart, and arranging them as the design indicates.

The straight braid is used for the flowers, and is arranged to form petals, the centres of which are filled in with cross bars. Any of the various lace stitches can be used for filling in the design.

After the work is completed remove it from the pattern, cutting away the surplus muslin, and press carefully with a warm iron.

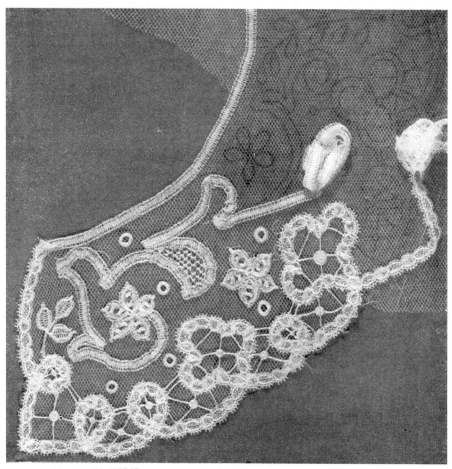

A CORNER OF THE COLLAR.

Carrickmacross Lace.

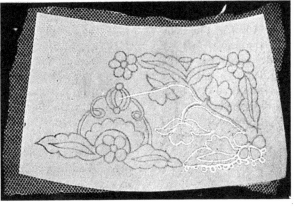

Showing how the couching is done, after net and muslin are tacked over the design.

Carrickmacross lace, as its name denotes, is especially an Irish lace. It has known many vicissitudes, but has survived them, and is even more popular to-

FLOWERETS DESIGN.

day than ever. This lace is exceedingly beautiful, and, at the same time, so simple of execution that those who are not great workers can, by a little care and

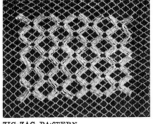

ZIG-ZAG PATTERN.

Some of the Lace Stitches that can be used.

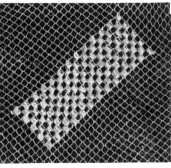

SIMPLE DARNED STITCH.

neatness, make handsome and valuable lace.

Materials required.

These are few, but should be of the best quality. They are Carrickmacross muslin, white or

DOTS AND RUNNING STITCHES.

cream; Brussels net, square mesh, white or cream; lace scissors, with bulb on one point; needles, sizes 10 and 12; design; Carrickmacross cotton,

A Section of a Carrickmacross Lace Collar.

The top illustration shows how the work is started.

Carrickmacross Lace.

white or cream, 60, 80, 150, 200.

To commence the work, first lay the net on the design, and then the muslin, tacking through all these round and across, and then very carefully round the design, avoiding the actual lines of the pattern. This tacking is very essential, as it greatly improves the finish of the lace.

Working the Design.

The worker must next find on her design a pattern where she can commence to work that will follow on as far as possible without breaking the

cord, the 60 and 150 cotton work well together, or the 80 and 200. The coarser thread is for the top cord, the finer for the sewing over. Commence by putting down a long thread, and then with the finer thread sew the coarse thread with small slanting whipping-stitches to both muslin and net. This is called "couching."

Avoid cutting the outlining thread as much as possible by turning back and sewing the two threads together if necessary. It will be noticed that the thread is usually turned into a picot at the edges. This is done by turning

A ROBESPIERRE COLLAR.

THE FINISHED WORK IS
VERY EFFECTIVE.

a loop on the thread, and securing it in place with a couple of neat stitches in the centre.

After a sufficiently long piece is worked, then cut out. This, of course, must be very carefully done, as the muslin must be cut away from the outside design, so as not to cut the net underneath. First pick up a little piece of muslin, and then cut round the pattern, keeping the blunt side of the scissors against the net. The spaces can then be filled in with fancy stitches. Some of these are here illustrated. After the work is finished, take off the pattern and press with a warm iron, putting some thin material between the iron and the work.

The designs for collars, etc., can, of course, be bought on glazed linen or ready traced on Carrickmacross muslin. Or if you prefer to use your own design, you should copy it on a piece of stiff white paper, such as drawing paper. Then go over it with pen and ink, rather heavily, and remove all trace of lead pencil carefully by rubbing with dry bread crumbs.

Where to get Materials.

This work makes beautiful collars, cuffs, scarf ends, fans, d'oilies, handkerchiefs, lace, etc., and one of the illustrations shows a corner of a beautiful "Robespierre" collar.

You can get this design, also the pattern of lace illustrated and all the requisites for this work, from Mr. William Barnard, 126, Edgware Road, London, W.; also a large number of other designs for this handsome form of work.

Bulgarian Embroidery.

There is a great demand for Bulgarian embroidery at present, for ornamenting collars, trimming coats and bodices, as well as for trimming hats. The Bulgarian women are famous for the embroideries with which they adorn their clothes and household napery. This embroidery is very easily made on coarse linen of an open texture, such as is at present used to form collars to wear with the coat or blouse.

Any design may be copied and the outline worked with stem stitch, as this must resemble a cord as closely as possible, then the centre may be

There is generally a fancy stitch used as an edging for insertion strips. In the samples shown, the first is worked in the fashionable shades of ecru and white on coarse linen, following the lines in the material the design is outlined with stem stitch over four threads, there are three

A VANDYKE PATTERN IN ECRU AND WHITE.

rows in each line, the two outside being in ecru and the centre white.

The edging is simply a straight stitch over two threads, leaving two between the stitches, then a row of square back stitch worked thus :—Make a horizontal back stitch over two threads, cross over two threads above these two and make another back stitch, this gives two sides of a square, make a back stitch over next two threads after the first, then another after the second and so on, working these two rows to the end, then return and work the other two sides of the square in the same way.

A DIAMOND INSERTION IN THREE SHADES.

filled in with any stitch with which you are familiar, such as flat stitch, stroke stitch, cross stitch, fishbone stitch, herring-boning, etc. The outline only may be done, according to the character of the design, or a portion of it filled, or entirely worked over.

The second sample is also worked in stem stitch in three shades, green, tan, and white. The tan color is worked first in a simple design of diamond shape, inside this there are three rows of white, all worked in the same way, then one of green, leaving the centre unworked. Outside the tan row there is one of white, then another of green. In the half-diamond space there is a vacant row after the green followed by a small green angle. A row of square back stitch finishes each edge.

This embroidery will be very fashionable for trimming linen costumes the coming summer, and as the machine-made kind cannot at all equal that made by hand, there is an opportunity for everyone to make her own trimming in this lovely fancy-work. The chief beauty of it lies in an artistic blending of color, vivid tones of purple, green and crimson, are blended with blue very effectually by separating the shades with a row of black. Ecru and all yellow shades are combined with white for the quieter kinds, and for evening wear, gold and silver threads are much used, combined with other colors which must match or contrast with the dress worn.

For trimming the collar and cuffs of a tweed costume or other material in which the threads cannot be counted, the design must be transferred to the material. It is then an easy matter to work the outline with regular stitches and fill in the design as already explained. For this purpose too, the outline may be made of fine braid and then the colored thread fills in the rest of the design.

Vegetable silk or any of the mercerised cottons may be used, as well as fine woollen thread and ordinary embroidery silk.

For washing materials Ardern's " Star Sylko " is very suitable.

Ribands for trimming hats are easily worked with the aid of a good transfer design. Choose a detached spray, and keep the remainder of the riband covered while working each, in order to avoid soiling the work.

A Linen Cover for a tea cosy ornamented with Bohemian Lace.

The herringbone stitches in the lace combine well with drawn work.

Limerick Tambour Lace.

Limerick "tambour" lace is suitable for collars, handkerchief borders and jabots, as well as for trimming evening dresses, etc. This lace is very easy to make, as it is composed almost entirely of the ordinary crochet chain stitch worked through the meshes of the net. A pattern of the design is essential, and this may be drawn on a sheet of white paper with pen and ink, or any transfer design can be employed, provided the motif contains continuous lines. The best Brussels net, a small tambour frame, a fine crochet-hook, Manlove's No. 60 and No. 100 Irish Lace Thread, and an ordinary fine sewing-needle are the materials required. The net is tacked carefully over the design, then with the finer thread the design is traced by running the stitches in and out through the meshes over the lines in the design, going over the outline only. Trace a line for the edges at both sides. Remove the net from the design by cutting the threads on the back of the paper, pick out the loose bits of thread, and arrange the net in the tambour frame.

With a crochet-hook make a loop on the end of No. 60 thread as if for a crochet chain, withdraw the hook and hold this loop with the fingers of the left hand under the frame up to the point in the design where you wish to begin, holding the tambour between the thumb and forefinger. With the crochet-hook in the right hand, insert it down through the mesh over the loop and draw the loop up to the right side, insert the hook through the next mesh (over the lines throughout) and draw up a loop of the thread, pull this loop through the loop on the hook, insert the hook through the next mesh and draw up a loop, then pull this through the loop on the needle, and so on.

This is the entire stitch, and only requires a very little practice to make one proficient. Having gone over the outlines, the centres of the leaves and petals are filled in with a couple of rows, using the finer thread, or the inside may be filled with fancy lace stitches. Scrolls are usually made solid, that is, close rows of the ch stitch are worked into them. The edges are then worked with a row, having a second row worked right through the centre of the first, the net is next cut away from the lower edge, and the lace placed between the folds of a piece of damped calico, press with a hot iron until the calico be dry, remove

A very Handsome Handkerchief Border which is not difficult to make.

the calico, and finish off on the back of the lace itself, when it is completed.

This Limerick Tambour Lace is often finished with a row of pearl edging sold for the purpose. This is top-sewn to

A SIMPLE LACE PATTERN.

the edge, using the finer thread.

To make the edges of the lace more durable it is usual to work a double row of ch around the edges, then cut away the net from outside the design, allowing a margin of two rows of meshes outside the outer line ; these rows are twirled under when sewing on the edging. For the handkerchief border, the inner edge is top-sewn to the lawn centre, allowing the two rows of margin, and twirling these when sewing on the wrong side to the hemstitching.

Limerick "Run" Lace.

Limerick "Run" Lace is one of the most expensive of the Irish laces. Exquisitely dainty in appearance and extremely fine in texture it requires the very best and finest of net made specially for the purpose. The design is placed under the net and the outline gone over with running stitch through the meshes. For this purpose very fine thread, Limerick Lace Thread No. 250 is used doubled. The single thread is employed for darning the meshes within the design, running the threads through the meshes first in one direction and then across. Any lace stitch may be used for the filling, and as a general rule the background is left clear. A fine pearl edging sold for the purpose is usually sewn round the edges of this lace to finish it. The pretty design illustrated would be suitable for a hand-kerchief border, or would make a delight-ful cor-ner for a square collar.

A PRETTY CORNER DESIGN.

My Workbox.

BY THE EDITOR.

THE WORK-BOX.

My interest in workboxes dates back to the time when I first read *The Wide Wide World*, and that was —well, it was the first long story book that I possessed for my very own! Up to that time, my personal library had consisted of children's coloured toy books, fairy tales and the like. The addition of *The Wide Wide World* (with roses and forget-me-nots on the cover) marked a distinct epoch in my life !

It was after I had read that enthralling chapter, where Ellen goes to the store with her mother and buys delightful things, and a workbox is among the parcels sent home, that I set to and tidied up the small wooden box (and a very inferior bit of furniture I felt it was, too, after the delightful affair Mrs. Mont-

gomery bought for *her* daughter!) thereby raising great hopes in the feminine portion of my older relatives. They trusted it was an indication that I was going to turn over a new leaf, and be more diligent with my needle ; alas ! it was nothing of the sort. As a small girl I detested needlework, and as a big girl I was vastly superior to everything of the kind. Plain needlework I felt was so sordid ; and fancy needlework so inane and futile!

When I was in my early teens I was quite convinced that I owed it to the world at large, to say nothing of posterity, to devote my intellect to far weightier matters and deeper matters than anything connected with needlework ; so you can see that the hopes of my elders

The article on the left is for a small spool of silk. The next is a carved screw for holding material firmly to the edge of a table. The centre article has a tape and measure at the top, bees-wax below, and a pincushion at its base. The next is a tape measure, and the ivory box on the right holds glove buttons. The carving on the ivory in each case is very fine.

were but short-lived. The only reason I tidied up my old work-box was because I was convinced that that perfect child, Ellen Montgomery, always kept hers scrupulously tidy; and as I was modelling myself entirely on her lines, naturally I felt

A Fancy Holder for a reel of cotton. The top is mother-of-pearl. The Ivory Mallet is a pin-cushion.

I was bound to pay attention to every small detail.

🞉 🞉

One of the humours of life as we grow older and leave our teens behind, is to look back and remember what self-opinionated little importances we were at about sixteen! How fixed were our views of life! How we knew everything! How certain we were that our ideas would be precisely the same for all the rest of time! And how original and wonderful we considered those ideas of ours to be! (and, incidentally, what a trial most of us were to our families at just about that age!)

This Crimson Silk Pin-cushion has groups of flowers and fruit finely carved in ivory on each side.

Still, it's a merciful thing that in the majority of cases we gain a little wisdom as we grow older, and learn that there may, after all, be some worth in the things we scorned as youngsters. It's a good thing, too, that our tastes often become quite healthy and normal as we proceed along the "twenties." It was so in

A round Pin-cushion with Chinese carving on the top. The small barrel is a tape measure.

my own case, I believe; for it was just about then that I began to develop an interest in needlework. It came to me as a sort of reaction after too much mental work, and the inevitable nervous breakdown that finds out most girls who are imbued with the notion that their intellectual attainments are of vast importance to the nation!

And after the breakdown, when I couldn't bear the sight of books or the sound of music, I found myself actually doing needlework, and liking it too; and the fascination of it grew upon me very rapidly, till now—I really don't know what I should do if I hadn't needlework to fall back upon, as a recreation, when I get overdone with the wear and tear and strain of work in our great city.

I always feel sorry for the business woman who hasn't found out what a charm and solace there is in doing sewing or crochet work, or knitting, or embroidery, after a day spent in wrestling with the stern commercial side of life. She misses so much.

But to return to the subject of work-boxes. By the time I found out for

The Editor's Work-box.

myself what a vast amount of pleasure can be produced by a ball of crochet cotton and a hook, my old work-box was no longer in existence.

A Wooden Case for packets of needles, brown ornamented with gilt.

I made shift with a work-basket and similar frauds, till at last it was borne in upon me that I must have a work-box, and a very comprehensive one too. I had all sorts of oddments in the way of fittings, and I got tired of rattling them about in an incapable work-basket, and diving for them to the bottom of a much-tangled-up work-bag.

I wandered around the shops, but the work-boxes they showed me seemed curiously inadequate in every particular—there was no room for anything in most of them, and they were singularly uninteresting as a whole in their appearance.

Beeswax, mounted with mother-of-pearl.

Nothing so convinces you that you want and must have a thing, as the fact that you can't get it! and by this time, all my spare moments seemed occupied with a craving for a nice work-box,

A mother-of-pearl and gilt thimble holder.

I even started to design one at last, only the design was never finished, because I could not make up my mind as to the exact number of compartments I should require.

Fortunately, when my need was becoming most acute, someone sent me a present of a box, that not only had as many compartments as I had longed for, but ever so many to spare; moreover, the box was so beautiful in itself, that it was, and still is a constant joy just to look at it.

This box is antique, and was evidently made in the East. So solid is it, that it is almost as heavy as a sewing machine to lift; but it stands always on a convenient side table, so its weight does not worry me. It is inlaid most exquisitely with ivory, tortoise shell,

This ancient little Dutch Doll is an Emery Bag.

silver, in addition to light and dark wood; the workmanship of the whole is wonderful. There are twenty-three roomy compartments in the top tray, and vast space below.

At last I had a respectable box for my many oddments; and it was not long before the collection grew; friends contributed items; relations turned out ancient put-away work-boxes and found little fittings which

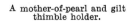

52

A Needle-case covered with blue, green, red, and white beads.

they sent me. And in a very little time it transpired that I had a work-box that was really something worth caring for and cherishing. The hobby has grown till now my work-box stands for all sorts of pleasant memories, and I can see myself in my old age getting quite garulous over it!

Now for the contents. There are tiny pin cushions of various kinds, round, square and heart shape, some of ivory and silk, with the finest of Chinese carving on the top. A carved ivory box holds small glove buttons.

The little Brass Bear.

There are quaint long needle-cases, some are carved, one very uncommon one is of bone, covered with a fine network of beads, these hold silver bodkins, beautifully engraved. Tape measures appear in various forms and unwind themselves either from a barrel, or by turning the tail of a donkey, from the top of a kind of pepper-box lighthouse. This last is a noble ornament, because, in addition to the tape measure, it provides a pin·cushion at its base,

and a piece of wax for waxing your thread, half way up.

There are quite a number of ornamental devices for holding bees-wax, some with silver ends, one with mother-of-pearl outside. Emery-bags also prevail, one taking the form of a charming little Dutch woman in a full green silk skirt. This is well over 60 years old.

There are needle books with various

A pair of Silver Scissors.

appropriate mottoes, such as "A stitch in time saves nine," a little wooden case for holding packets of needles, one or two carved wooden boxes for hooks and eyes, a pearl thimble case, an old-time "housewife," a little brass bear with a head that lifts up and makes room for darning needles inside him. (By the way, he is evidently the twin brother to the little brass bear described by Mrs. Barclay in *The Rosary.*)

Perforated cardboard was much patronized by our grandmothers. Among other things, I have an ornamental case for holding court plaster, made with perforated cardboard worked in red and blue silk. On one side are the appropriate words—

A Carved Needle-case.

The Editor's Work-box.

Go, little case,
Thy kind assistance lend,
And cure when cut
The finger of my friend.

while on the back is worked—
Oh may you never, never feel
A deeper wound than this can heal.

Devices for holding silk when wound were more popular in the past, when silk was dear and mercerised cottons were unknown. My work-box contains both wooden and mother-of-pearl silk winders, and a little carved silk holder, with a top that unscrews and a small hole at the side for the silk strand to come through.

Gentlewomen of the bye-gone age evidently indulged in note books as pretty as any to be found to-day. I have an ancient note-book containing paper and an ivory tablet. The binding outside is dark leather stamped very ornately with gold. In the centre, both back and front, is let in a medallion of the very finest Berlin wool work I have ever seen. Each medallion shows a group of roses and foliage perfectly executed. Yet is not more than an inch and a half across. The book inside is gorgeous with rose-silk pockets. In a flowing Italian hand, that so well matches the period of the book, someone has written down notes of a sermon preached at Cheltenham, but no date appears (a truly feminine omission!) It is possible that the same lady owned the flat silver vinaigrette, opening like a snuff box, that I keep in one compartment, with similar relics. It seems to suggest a hot day in church.

But the work-box is practical as well as ornamental. It is a matter of puffed up pride with me that I can invariably supply everybody's needs in the way of haberdashery.

There are linen buttons of all the orthodox sizes; glove and shoe buttons galore; hooks and eyes, white and black, of all gardes; cottons and silks for mending every imaginable shade of gloves, with lots of dress colours thrown in; white embroidery threads and cotton lie in orderly skeins, from size 1 onwards.

Friends try to catch me napping, and come to ask me for things they think I shan't have in stock, but I can usually supply them. White elastic I was asked for recently, also narrow linen tape, and black velvet binding for a skirt-bottom, I produced them all, trying to look modest, though I knew the inquirer didn't really need them. I told her I could also supply frilled elastic for suspenders if she required any, and small brass or ivory rings for sewing on fancy bags, and pins with any colour heads she liked to name. She retired, duly discomfited I trust.

Now my reason for telling about my work-box is to suggest to any readers who have only regarded a work-box as an uninteresting necessity that they might do worse than develop a "work-box hobby." I really do not know of many things that are more fascinating in a feminine way.

There is something very pretty about a well-ordered work-box, to start with, and that in itself is a great advantage. I like to look at the rainbow-coloured silks and cottons, at the lengths of pretty narrow ribbon for lingerie, at the gay little pincushions, and the tiny bags made from odd bits of flowery silk, that I

use for special buttons.
And then the utility
of it gives an added
charm. There is the
same sort of pleasure
in keeping it properly
stocked as there is
in looking after the
st o r e - c u p b o a r d,
Moreover, this is not
an expensive hobby.
One can add a few
reels of cotton at a time, and
it does not amount to so very
much.

A Box of Ribbon and Perforated
Cardboard, ornamented with a
wreath of forget-me-nots and
roses.

The fittings, again,
seem to collect them-
selves. Once you start,
you will be surprised to
find how many trifles
turn up that you
pounce upon at once,
exclaiming, "That will
just do for my work-
box!" Whether the
things are mordern or
antique matters little,
so long as they are pretty in themselves
and can be turned to some practical
purpose.

Making Bohemian Lace.

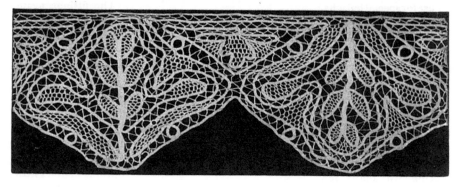

The novelty of this lace lies in its simplicity of design and execution.

The design must form a series of curves, in fact, any simple braiding pattern can be followed for this make of lace, so long as sharp corners are avoided as much as possible.

Materials required : A very narrow lace braid, or even tape of the narrowest make will answer the purpose, though the lace braid is finer. Tack the braid carefully over your pattern. Fill in the spaces by taking a thread from one side of the braid to the other as for herring-boning, but fastening the thread each time with a sort of knot formed thus : Hold down the 2 strands of thread with the thumb, make a button-hole stitch over these 2 strands. Draw up tightly, thus forming a kind of knot. Continue on opposite side the same.

To form a variety, the stitches are made more closely together in the narrow spaces, and the very wide spaces are filled in in the same manner, with a simple lace or button-hole stitch.

In the more elaborate designs, button-holed bars fill in the very wide spaces.

This make of lace is most effective for infants' garments, lingerie frocks, jabots, and collars.

It also has a handsome effect when let into table linen of a fine quality.

This could be inserted in the end of a Sideboard Cloth, or in a linen Tea Cosy Cover, as illustrated on page 47.

The Educational Value of the Doll.

The educational value of the Doll is just beginning to be realized by the mothers and teachers of small girls; so that at last we have the making of doll's clothes included in the curriculum of certain schools.

This is undoubtedly a step in the right direction. The little girl who

when she in turn has little people to sew for. In the same way, the small girl who has been shown how to bring Lady Arabella's "last season's party frock" up-to-date, by altering the sleeves, or the fulness of the skirt — as the latest mode may demand — will save many a dress-

An Insertion with only simple stitches

An Edge in Bohemian Lace, showing buttonholed bars.

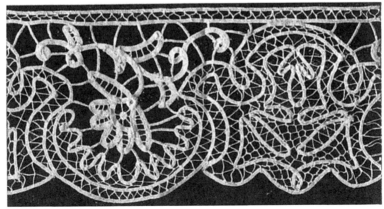

has taken a part in making her doll's wardrobe, and then in keeping it up-to-date, will find that the knowledge she has gained in this way will be invaluable to her in after life. The child who has helped to put together her doll's combinations, will have no difficulty in making her own later on, neither will she be perplexed

maker's bill presently, when her own frocks show signs of growing out-of-date.

But this instruction as to the doll's wearing apparel is only the beginning of the educational possibilities of the doll. The next step is to encourage the little girl to see to the household linen and general furnishings of the

doll's house. If a real doll's house
is not forthcoming at the moment, an
excellent substitute can be made out
of a wooden box turned up on end,
with a few shelves put in to supply
the necessary succession of "floors."
Once you have contrived something
that you can call a doll's house—and
the child's innate love of "make
believe" will enable you to do this
easily—doll's furniture can be
procured at very little cost, and the
etceteras can be supplied by your own
ingenuity.

First the bedclothes and bedding
should be made. It will be best for
the child if you make all this your-
selves, rather than buy the small
bolster and pillows at the toy shop.

Show her how to make the small
feather bed, and how to stuff the
pillows. She can make a little
mattress from small cloth clippings;
this will teach her the value of tiny
waste bits of material. Have everything as complete as you can, from
the under blanket to the ornamental
bedspread; and show her how to
make the bed in a proper way. A
valance will be received with accla-
mation, and you can show her how
to fasten it on with tapes.

A nightdress pocket is sure to
delight any little maid; and in using
it for Lady Arabella's elegant night-
gown, she will learn, unconsciously,
what she must do with her own.

A little Linen Bag can also be made
to serve a useful purpose; and if Lady
Arabella is always taught to put dis-
carded garments in her Linen Bag,
preparatory to sending them to the
wash, the other little lady will be
learning tidy methodical ways at the
same time.

Doll's cupboards can be bought at

most toy shops for a few pence; turn
one of these into a linen press, and
have it furnished under your super-
vision with tablecloths, serviettes, tray-
cloths, towels and toilet covers, as well
as with bed linen. Shew the little
housewife how to ornament the guest
towels, how to fold the serviettes and
tablecloths correctly, how to put a bit
of edging round the toilet covers and
tray cloths, and how to let in a fancy
corner into the 5 o'clock tea-cloth.
If she is old enough to do some of the
ornamentations for herself, so much
the better; let her try to do a very
simple cross-stitch border round a
sideboard cloth for Lady Arabella's
dining room; any coarse piece of
canvas will serve, so long as the
cotton is a pretty colour.

In this way you will not only be
instilling in your child a love of
housewifely things, and fostering the
instinct for home-making that is born
in most baby girls, but you will be
teaching her the right way to do
things, and what is required in a
properly conducted household; also,
you will be training her to make the
things she needs. And none of this
need be any tax on the brain. It will
all be absorbed with the utmost
delight, as play.

But do not misunderstand me. I
am not advocating that the mother
should invariably supervise the child's
play.

I think a child should be allowed
the old-time freedom in this respect:
the modern custom of helping or
training or assisting a child to play
only tends to dwarf its self reliance
and stunt its ingenuity. But while
the little girl has plenty of time to
amuse herself with the doll's house
as she pleases, it is easy for the mother

to get in her instructions by the way. She can announce that she is going to pay a ceremonious visit to Lady Arabella, and the house must be put in applepie order for the occasion. Then the guest towels can be hanging over the towel horse: fresh covers on the drawing-room cushions, the best bedspread over the bed, and the serviettes in their bead-rings round the dining-room table.

Having the child make the house and bed linen teaches her how to sew with very little irksomeness. Each article is so small that it can be quickly finished, and is not like the large pieces of work that were given children to do a generation ago. Few children can get up any enthusiasm

over hemming a duster! But it will be the exceptional girl who is not eager to hem the small sheet for the doll's bed and put a piece of lace at the edge; and if mother can find— or evolve—a monogram or initial for the pillow-case, needlework will take on an added delight in the eyes of the small person. To learn to make a buttonhole properly is dull work for a young girl, yet it is necessary, as we most of us need this knowledge as we grow older; but if she learns the stitch in the first instance by buttonholing the top of the doll's blanket a bright blue or red, she will be acquiring useful information as well as a good deal of pleasure in doing this piece of work.

For a Curtain Border.

Darned filet net is one of the most artistic forms of fancy-work. It is always in fashion and affords ample scope for one's own designing, which can be carried out to our own ideas of the manner in which it should be worked. Simple darning stitch is used, in which the thread is run in and out through the meshes in sufficient rows to fill a line of the meshes in any direction required. The outline of the motif is worked in this way with soft embroidery cotton, then additional value is assured to the work by "filling in" with any fancy stitches with which we are acquainted. This design, while suggested for a curtain border, will also serve for an insertion border for a tea-cloth. cushion-cover, or it could be adapted for a delightful cot-cover over a pink or blue satin lining.

For this purpose a centre motif, or a group of them, such as that in the corner could be put in the centre of the cover.

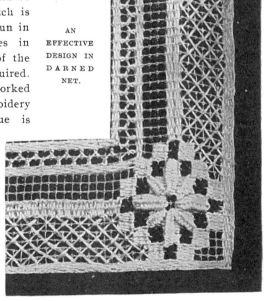

AN EFFECTIVE DESIGN IN DARNED NET.

A Lesson in Hemstitching.

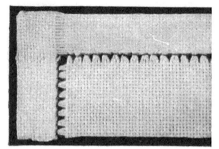

Fig. 1.—SIMPLE HEMSTITCHING.

The best finish for all kinds of work that require frequent washing is the hemstitched hem. This can be of various depths, and either plain hemstitching or very elaborate work of the "drawn thread" kind, with fancy stitchery. Linen sheets and pillow-cases afford samples of articles

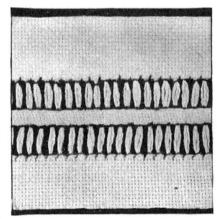

Fig. 8.—DOUBLE LADDER STITCH.

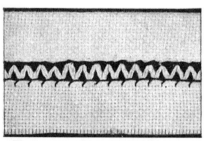

Fig. 5.—THE SERPENTINE STITCH.

which are improved by a deep hem ornamented with some openwork veining. Coloured embroidery cottons or white are used with good effect, and the number of stitches that can be employed is indefinite.

For all hemstitching a number of threads, depending upon the width of openwork liked, must be drawn from the material immediately under the edge of the hem.

In Fig. 1, which shows plain hemstitching, 4 threads only were drawn. Mark the depth of the hem required and draw out the 4 threads below the line where the edge of the hem is to be. Turn down the hem and tack it in place. With the embroidery cotton or linen thread, and an ordinary sewing needle, commence by fastening the thread to the end of the hem with a few stitches, at the left side, * slip the needle in from right to left under 3 of the threads, draw it out and put the needle upwards through the edge of the hem under the 2nd horizontal thread, * repeat.

Some people work from right to left of the hem. In this case the working thread is held in a loop with the left thumb, while passing the needle under the fabric threads, and the needle brought out through the loop.

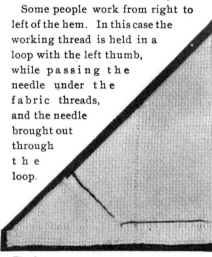

Fig. 2.—SHOWING HOW TO TURN A CORNER.
The black line along the bottom is merely the end of the cotton.

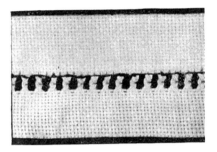

Fig. 3.—TWISTED OPENWORK BARS.

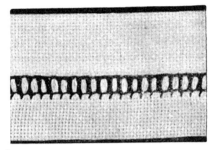

Fig. 4.—THE LADDER STITCH.

Figure 2 shows how to turn a corner for this plain hemstitching. You mark lines for the hem and draw the threads as before, then fold the material diagonally through the corner as in the illustration. This gives you a small triangle in the corner. Fold back the diagonal edge of the triangle to get the half of it and crease along this line. N o w back-stitch along the creased line down to where you turn in the edge of the hem. Cut away the corner outside the seam,

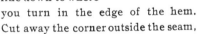

Fig. 9.—WRONG SIDE OF DOUBLE
LADDER STITCH.

which you fold down flat, turn this corner section inside out and you have a neat line on the wrong side of your hem going diagonally from the corner to the edge of the hem.

Figure 3 shows this hem with a row of stitching which twists the openwork bars. Proceed as before with the hem, but take an even number of threads with each stitch ; in this case 4 were taken. Fasten the thread to the end of the openwork at the left, *insert the needle after the next 4th thread,

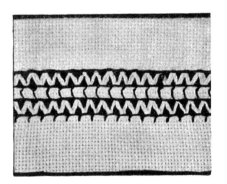

Fig. 6.—DOUBLE SERPENTINE STITCH.

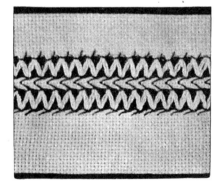

Fig. 7.—WRONG SIDE OF DOUBLE
SERPENTINE STITCH.

and turning the point backwards to left again bring it up under the 3rd and 4th threads, over the 2nd and 1st, twist the needle round underneath this group and bring it up again after the 4th thread, * repeat.

Figure 4 shows the hemstitching worked at both sides of the openwork. This is known as the ladder-stitch and is worked the same at both sides; instead of putting the thread through the edge of the hem at the other side you put it under the 2nd horizontal thread in the edge of the material.

Figure 5.—The serpentine stitch, for which a greater number of theads are drawn, eight being taken out for the sample. An even number of threads is necessary. Hemstitch with 4 threads, then at the other side hemstitch in the same way, but take the last half of the 1st group with the 1st half of the 2nd, and so on.

Figure 6.—The double serpentine stitch. Here 2 groups of thread are drawn, leaving a plain strip of material between them. Draw 8 threads, leave 4, draw 8. Hemstitch the top row and the lower edge, then hemstitch at the sides next to the plain strip, but instead of putting the needle through the material take a stitch at each side alternately.

Figure 7 shows the wrong side of this hem.

Figure 8.—These are plain bars worked as in Fig. 4, but with a plain strip as in No. 7, which is worked in the same way.

Figure 9 shows the wrong side of Fig. 8.

A Good Finish for Canvas Work.

Fold canvas back as far as work is to go that there may be the firmness of double material for the long stitches. The illustration will show the working of alternate colours.

Place a netting mesh of ivory or steel, sometimes wood, even with the edge. Take a threaded rug needle over this from each hole in

the canvas 10 times. Next the other needleful of second colour 10 times. When the mesh is full, the upper part can be made from 9 threads.

Make 9 stitches of graduated lengths, the longest one 9 threads high, cross

corners. These should be the same colour as the tassel. The shorter and more open threads the reverse way are the colour of the next tassel, the centre longest one first, three each side, leaving a clear opening between each two.

The mesh can now be drawn from through the loops along it. Wind round and cut once 20 strands of each colour, place a short length of the thread through the loops and hold the cut ends taut to them and tie tight through the middle, pulling down firm, and afterwards clipping even.

The Marguerite Glove and Handkerchief Sachet.

The accompanying illustrations show something quite new in the way of decorating a glove and handkerchief sachet. The very realistic marguerites are made by covering a shilling-sized button mould with satin, silk or sateen, and then sewing on to the wrong side, some old-fashioned white vandyke braid. This braid should be put on with an "oversew" stitch, point by point, pushing each as closely together as possible.

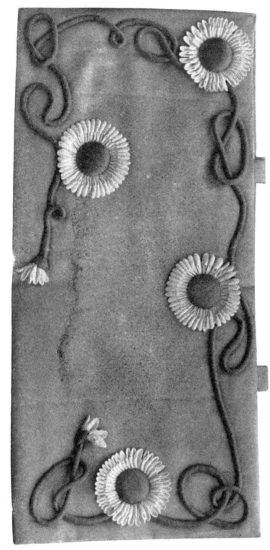

THE GLOVE SACHET.

When finished a running thread should be placed through the centre of the braid, right round the circle, in order to keep each "petal" in position.

The vandyke braid used in these designs is three-quarters of an inch in depth.

The buds consist of six points of braid gathered tightly together, and enclosed in a little silk calyx. The raw edges should be turned inwards, and running stitches used top and bottom.

The tubular cord representing the braiding stems is made by covering ordinary cord with silk or satin. As this is sometimes rather stiff, however, instead of using the soft cord, three or four strands of wool will be found much easier, as it will turn and twist more satisfactorily. After preparing the cord, place it carelessly on the sides of the sachet, turn it at intervals, and tie a loose knot or two. Let it " wiggle " itself into a pattern.

The sachets are made in the usual

The Marguerite Handkerchief Sachet.

way by covering fairly stiff book muslin with a thin layer of wadding, then tacking over the outer side, sateen or silk. Work all the outside decoration next so that the stitches can be taken right through, and finally line the inside. The fastenings on these satchets are made by inserting little stiffened silk tabs between the outer cover and inside lining, and sewing on ordinary spring punch buttons.

This handkerchief sachet is made in the same way as the glove sachet.

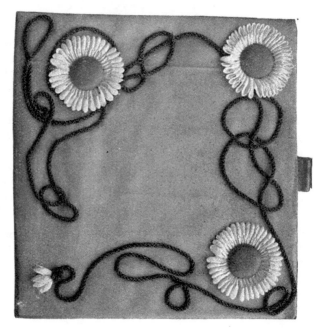

The only difference is that ordinary cord is used, and not the tubular cord.

FOR THOSE INTERESTED IN HIGH-CLASS NEEDLECRAFT

The following volumes have been issued uniform with this series, in the same style, on art paper, and high-class reproduction.

THE HOME ART CROCHET BOOK, containing designs for edgings, insertions, tray cloth borders, etc.

THE HOME ART BOOK OF FANCY STITCHERY, dealing with a variety of forms of work, including Drawn Thread Work, Resille Net, Bead Work, Hedebo Embroidery, Cut Work, etc.

THE CRAFT OF THE CROCHET HOOK, giving a lesson in Plain Crochet and Irish Crochet, and containing some very novel ideas for crochet workers.

THE MODERN CROCHET BOOK, containing new and unusual ideas for use on Household Linen, Underwear, etc.

All these volumes are edited by **FLORA KLICKMANN.**

Price **1**/- net.

Beads and Bead=work.

The woman for whom beads have no attraction is not easy to find. An admiration for beads is a characteristic of women of most nationalties. In the present day it is possible to get some really beautiful beads, and they can be used in so many different ways that delightful necklaces and chains can be made. Some of the season's novelties are really lovely. A few are illustrated here, but in pictures of this kind it is quite impossible to portray the beauty of the beads. Still, with some little description, these will give an idea of what can be obtained and made.

The necklace shown at the top of this page is made of Venetian beads of a lovely shade of Turquoise, interspersed with gold filigree beads, the tiny beads being of metal, the same shade as the Venetian. As will be seen from the illustration, a double

OF TURQUOISE VENETIAN AND GOLD FILIGREE BEADS.

row of small beads is used for the upper portion, but after being threaded through the long bead on each side, the threads divide, and a pendant effect is given. A chain of this description is not at all difficult to make.

Another illustration shows a very effective necklace made of two kinds of Venetian beads, the dark ones being black covered with exquisite little coloured flowers, while the lighter ones are of crystal and gold, with spots of pink. Between are gold torse beads and gold glass bugles. The chain is made on one thread only and is the simplest kind to make, and it is—as will easily be seen—most effective.

The little bracelet is made on two rows of bead wire, and is of Cats' Eyes (flat green beads) and small aluminium beads. A great advantage of these aluminium beads is that they

A MOST SIMPLE CHAIN TO MAKE.

The New Bead Necklaces.

will not tarnish. These beads are, of course, equally suitable for necklaces and chains, and also for hair ornaments.

The largest illustration s h o w s several chains. A particularly pretty one is the second from the top. This is made of one of the prettiest kinds of beads—the medallion. This is a flat round bead, and one which is preferred by a good many, because it shows so prettily on the blouse. This particular chain is of an exquisite shade of blue, but these beads can be obtained in other shades. The small beads used here are silver metal beads, while at each side of the medallion bead is a gold torse bead.

The illustration immediately below the medallion necklace shows one made of Venetian beads, the particular attraction of which lies in the fact that no two Venetian beads used in its manufacture are alike. The connecting beads are small gold filigree (next to the Venetian beads) with gold metal beads in between.

A section of a long mosaic bead chain is shown under. This gives a pleasing example of how pretty a colour scheme may be obtained with fairly sombre shades. The actual mosaic bead—the large one—has tones of green, yellow, blue and white. * Next to it is a green bead, 2 small gold, 7 bronze, 2 gold. Then follow a brown bead the same size as the green referred to, 2 gold, 7 bronze, 1 gold, 52 tiny green metal beads, 1 gold, 7 bronze, 2 gold, 1 brown, 2 gold, 7 bronze, 2 gold, 1 green, 2 gold, 7 bronze, 2 gold, 1 green, 2 gold, 7 bronze, 2 gold, 1 brown, 2 gold, 7 bronze, 1 gold, 52 small green, 1 gold, 7 bronze, 2 gold, 1 brown, 2 gold, 7 bronze, 2 gold, 1 green, 1 mosaic. Repeat from *.

Those whose tastes run to more delicate productions, however, should see the Persian beads. A necklace of

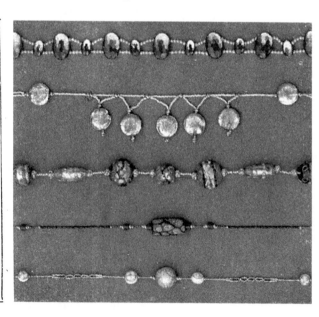

This shews a number of most effective necklaces and chains.

The design at the top is equally suitable for a Hair Bandeau.

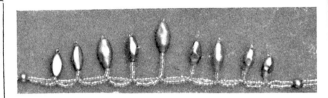

these is shown immediately below the mosaic chain. These beads can be obtained in various sizes and shapes, and show for the most part, beautiful pale shades on white grounds, giving the beads the appearance of delicate china. This particular necklace is made on two threads, which at intervals are divided and then connected again. The colours in this are Wedgewood blue, pale coral, silver and white, and it is quite impossible to describe the beauty of this attractive little article.

A BRACELET OF CATS' EYES
AND ALUMINIUM BEADS.

The top design shows a chain of two sizes of a beautiful amethyst bead, with small seed pearls between. These amethyst beads, like the Cat's Eyes, have two holes on each side, and therefore are always used with two rows of small beads. This fact, and the flat character of the beads, makes them very suitable for hair bandeaux, especially as this shape can be obtained in other colours. For instance, the kind known as Fire Opals look very lovely in the hair, also the Moonstone Jewels.

While on the subject of hair ornaments, the tiara shown is worth attention. It is made of Baroque Pearls (gold coloured long beads) with gold glass beads between. A point about these Baroque Pearls which makes them so useful for wearing in the hair is that they are exceedingly light in weight.

Hair bands can also be made with two sizes of pearl beads, a rather large size for the edges and smaller for the trellis-work between — the favourite mode. String the pearls on very fine wire, to be obtained at any large drapery shop (used for binding the stems of millinery flowers, principally). This wire is very fine and pliable, and can readily be "threaded" through the beads without the use of a needle. Make the 2 edges of the band first and secure both ends. Fasten the wire to the first bead and commence the trellis-work by threading as many beads as will go diagonally through what would be a square between the 2 edges, get the first line right and the rest cannot go wrong, for you simply thread the same number of beads each time and fasten by twining the wire around that in the outside rows between the 2 beads where the lines cross, going from one side to the other alternately, in right angles. According to the closeness of the lines, the number of beads between each diagonal line must be even, or divisible by 3. When the first row is finished, fasten the wire to the edge, after the second or third bead, and thread the same number as before and fasten after the second or third bead at the other side. Fill all the angles in this way, winding the wire once around each line that it crosses, keeping the number of beads at each side of the trellis equal. The ends of the band are generally finished with a large " cabachon " made with pearls or contrasting beads.

Net blouses for evening wear, spangled with beads, are also very easy to make. In Brussels net the meshes run in straight lines and in angles to each other, and it is an easy thing to form geometrical designs by simply following the lines in any way selected. The beads are fastened in place with a knot stitch for each, so that in the event of one getting pulled off, others near it may not fall off too, as is the case with the bought beaded net. Beaded fringes for edging draperies are so easily made that there is no need to describe them.

Then for belts, bags, etc., there is the apache bead work that any girl can easily make on the little loom made and sold for the purpose. This can be obtained from Mr. F. E. Rogier, 14, High Street, Kensington, London, W., with all the materials requisite. Here, too, can be had very large and varied selection of beads of every kind. He will send price lists, sample cards, etc., on approval.

A Bag to Match Your Costume.

In the present day a bag is no longer merely a bag, but it is a very important accessory to the well-dressed woman. The shape, style, and colour are carefully considered, with a view to suiting the costume with which it is to be used. Such a one can quite easily be made, and will give a very distinctive look. The bag here illustrated was made of satin of a pretty mole shade to match the dress of the wearer. The simple diagonal stitching was done in soft embroidery silk of the same colour, and at the points of intersection a coral bead was sewn. This touch of brighter colour matched the coral trimming in costume and hat. The cord and tassels were of the mole shade. A bag of this kind is quite simple to make, and practically any colour or material could be used.

A Hardanger Embroidery Cloth.

For this cloth a square of Hardanger or Congress Canvas of medium mesh is required, and the work is done in Faudel's Vivid Lustre for the solid work, and Faudel's Sylkoline for the weaving.

Commence the work about 6 inches middle of each. To turn the corner, work a 2nd row of blocks by the side of the upper half of the last diamond, which row forms the 1st side of the diamond for the 2nd side of the cloth. The blocks of the lower half of the 2 diamonds are continued in a straight

THE FINISHED CLOTH LOOKS VERY HANDSOME.

from the outside edge, and 120 threads from the middle of a side. Begin at the lowest point of the 1st diamond, and work 11 blocks of 5 stitches over 4 threads. Continue this up and down for the 4 diamonds, working the top halves to correspond, and leaving 4 threads between the 2 blocks in the line across the corner,—there must be an extra block worked in the space between the two halves of the last diamond, so that there will be 11 blocks on each side of this extra block in this straight row.

Continue the diamonds, 4 on each side, around the cloth, then work in

A Hardanger
Embroidery Cloth.

the small inner diamonds. These consist of 6 blocks at each side of the diamond, and care must be taken to work them exactly opposite the corresponding blocks in the outer diamonds, so that the threads are correct for the openwork. The crosses are then filled in, beginning in the centre hole, 6 stitches are taken on the diagonal, each stitch being raised a mesh, and the 2nd row of each point being taken into the same hole as the first. The eyelet holes are worked at each side in the space between the points.

Next fill in the triangles at the outside of the diamonds with halves of stars, making the stitches of the lower side level with the lowest block of the diamond. Fill in the single eyelet holes between the points of the star, and then work 4 eyelet holes together, making the inside stitches of all 4 meet in 1 hole, which forms a small hole in the centre.

Each side of the diamonds is next outlined with 3 rows of backstitching, making each row finish in the same row of the mesh as the lowest block of the diamond. An eight-pointed star is worked on the outside of each corner.

When the solid work is completed, the threads are cut for the woven and whipped bars, which are worked in the spaces between the inner and outer diamonds, the whipping and weaving being worked in alternate diamonds. For the woven bars the threads are cut at the sides of all the blocks, and those left are woven with a picot in the middle of each side of each bar. For the whipped bars there are more threads left than cut. They are cut at the side of the middle block of the inner diamond.

Leave uncut the next 2 sides of the blocks round the diamond, cut the sides of the next 2, leave uncut the sides of the end block, and repeat this

SHOWING HOW THE CORNER IS MANAGED.

THIS SHOWS THE DETAIL OF THE DIAMONDS.

scheme around the inner diamond. Then cut the same threads on the inside of the outer diamond, draw the threads and whip.

Next the 4 threads are drawn for the openwork rows at each side of the insertion, leaving 5 threads between the half stars and the 1st drawn thread.

At the inner side of the corner a set of 4 blocks must be arranged to hold the cut ends of these threads. This will not exactly fit into the double row of blocks in the corner, but the sides must be made to face the threads which are to be cut. The outside row must be held in some such way as is shown in the illustration, or it could be carried right across the hem. The threads are then worked in sets of 3 bars—a whipped one on each side of woven one, and the three are then drawn together by small stitches at the back. Except in very fine canvas, it will be found sufficient to whip 3 threads together, and weave two, as, if more are taken, the effect is clumsy when drawn together.

71

Braid Appliqué on Net.

Braid Appliqué affords an easy method for ornamenting the fine white net now so fashionable, and some of the designs here illustrated give some idea of the variety that can be obtained in this way. The braid is sewn on the wrong side to the net in any simple design, then the net may be pleated or tucked to form a frill, or the work may be—and very often is—further embellished by the addition of fine crochet.

In most of the designs shown, the tiny picot or Mignardise Braid (also known as a fine Cordon Braid) has been used in this way; while in one, a rather coarser braid has been used as well. In two of the corners, which would make handsome finishes for net curtains, fine Feather-stitched Braid has been employed. For blouse trimmings, jabots, collars, &c., Honiton Lace Braid can be used with remarkably good effect. Braid can

A HANDSOME LACE.

also be applied to cambric or table linen. ⌜Some⌝ of the illustrations show suitable sprays for this. Others will doubtless suggest themselves to the worker. Although the crochet is not necessary in every case, the work is improved by it, and we give directions for it.

A Handsome Lace.

In the wide lace on page 72 a flower spray of braid is shown, then as a finish, a narrow insertion at each side of a strip of the net is very appropriate. Lace frilling is attached to the insertion in which the pleats are sewn down in the form of tucks, three of which come down the centre of each vandyke.

For the Insertion.

Use two strips of the braid and fine crochet cotton, such as Perilusta No. 80. * Into each of 2 picots 1 d c, 5 ch, miss a picot, 3 tr into next, 5 ch, * repeat.

On the 2nd strip work the same on one side but fasten in the ch immediately before and after the 3 tr to the corresponding chs on the 1st strip.

At each of the outside edges put 1 ch, 1 d c into every picot.

The vandyke edging is worked in a similar way for the inside rows, but on the first strip * miss 5 picots after the 4th group of 3 tr, 1 ch, 3 tr into the 6th picot, then after the next 3rd group 5 ch, 2 d c (into 2nd and 3rd picots), 9 ch, 2 d c into next 2 picots, continue the 5 ch and groups of trs for 4 groups and repeat from * to the end.

Work the 2nd strip in the same way, commencing at the top of the vandyke and join as in the insertion.

For the top outside row 1 tr, 2 ch

into every picot, missing 5 picots in every point turned downwards and omitting the ch between the trs at each side.

The Lower Edging.

1st Row.—Commencing at the first upward point in the picot before the last group of 3 tr, on the other side of the braid put 2 tr, * miss 2 picots, 1 tr into next, 1 tr into each of next two 2nd picots, miss 2 picots, 2 tr into next, 3 ch, 2 tr into 2nd picot, 3 times, 4 ch, 2 tr into 2nd picot, 8 ch, miss 2 picots, 2 d c into next 2, 4 ch, 2 d c into 2nd next picot, 5 times, 8 ch, 2 tr into 3rd next picot, 4 ch, miss next picot, 2 tr into next, 3 ch, 2 tr into 2nd picot 3 times, then repeat from *.

2nd Row.—* Into each of the 3 spaces before the 8 ch loop 3 d c, 4 ch, 3 d c, 10 tr, 1 d c into next loop, 7 tr, 1 d c into each of the 5 ch loops, 10 tr, 1 d c into next, into each of next 3 spaces 3 d c, 4 ch, 3 d c, cross over to the opposite side with 10 ch. picot 5 of them, 5 ch, and repeat from *.

A Continuous Border.

Besides the two kinds of braid, Manlove's No. 42 Irish Lace Thread and some Breton Net are required for this design.

The Leaf Motif.

Using the coarser braid, commence about 1½ inches from the end of the braid in one of the tiny picots into which put a d c, 5 ch, picot 4 of them, 1 ch, 1 d c into next picot, miss next picot, 1 tr into next, miss next picot, 1 tr into next, 5 ch picot 4 of them, 1 d c into next picot, 7 ch, turn these back to the 1st loop and fasten with a d c, turn, over the 7 ch put 4 d c 5 ch 4 d c, * 1 d c into the braid picot,

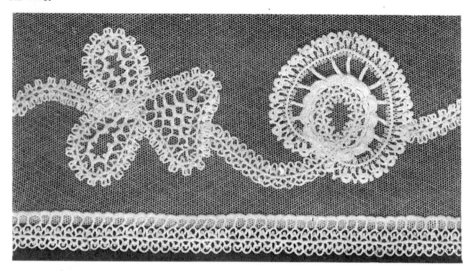

A CONTINUOUS BORDER.

5 ch picot 4 of them, 1 ch, 1 d c into next picot, 7 ch 1 d c into the picot on last bar, 7 ch 1 d c into next picot on braid, turn, over each of these bars put 4 d c 5 ch 4 dc, * repeat for 4 bars in the row.

Work a corner like the 1st, then connect the 4 d c bars with 3 ch to and from the picots in the bars and next 4 in the braid. Cross the ends of the braid and secure with a single stitch through the 2 together. Continue with the 2nd leaflet by 4 ch 1 d c into 2nd picot, 6 ch 1 d c into 3rd, 7 ch 1 d c into the 4th, 5th, 7th, 9th, 11th, and 13th picots, then 7, 6, 5, 4 ch into next 4 picots respectively. Cross over to the 1st loop into which put 4 d c, 4 d c 5 ch 4 d c into each of the others, ending with 4 d c into the last. Cross the braid, secure it as before, then bring it behind the centre leaflet and form the 3rd leaflet like the 2nd at the other side.

The braid is continued in the stem at each side of which there are * 2 d c worked on the edge of the loop, 4 ch 1 d c into the picot, 4 ch 2 d c on the other side of the loop *, repeat around the stem and all round each of the 3 leaflets.

The Oval Motif.

Cut off 7 inches of the coarser braid. Into each loop at each side of the picot put 1 tr with 6 ch between, for 14 loops, form the braid into a loop with these stitches on the outside of it, cross the braid and secure it. Over each 6 ch put 6 d c, 9 ch 1 d c into the d c between the loops in the preceding row. Into each 9 ch loop 1 d c, 9 tr.

Cross over behind the motif and taking up a piece of Mignardise braid join with a d c, 5 ch, 1 d c into the 9th picot on the braid, 1 d c into 1 d c into next picot, 5 d c over the 5 ch, 7 ch, 1 d c into the d c after the 9 tr on the centre, * 9 ch 1 d c into the 4th next loop on the braid, 1 d c into next loop, turn, 9 d c over the chs, 7 ch 1 d c into the d c after next 9 tr on the centre, * repeat all round, but after the 4th bar miss 4 picots on the braid instead of the 3 until the corresponding bars are reached at the other side, then finish as at the beginning. Sew

74

the ends of the braid securely behind the centre portion.

1st Outside Row.—2 d c into 1st 2 picots on the braid, * 5 ch 1 d c into next picot, 5 ch, 2 d c into next 2 picots * repeat all round.

2nd Row.—* 2 d c into top of 1st loop, 2 d c into next loop, 5 ch, turn back and fasten to the 2nd d c, into this loop put 5 d c, 1 d c into the 2nd loop in the 1st row, 5 ch picot 4 of them, 1 ch, * repeat into next loops.

Work the 3-inch stem on the coarser braid with the same row as the 1st on the centre at both sides of it.

The Edging.

This is simply the 1st outside row of the oval motif, repeated at both sides of the strip of coarser braid with a heading of 1 long tr, 5 ch into each loop, finish with a row of 5 d c into each space.

The motifs are tacked in position on the net, then sewn on the back of the work with fine thread.

A Pleated Net Design.

Use 2 lengths of braid at the same time. Into 1st braid make 1 d c, 6 ch, 1 d c into each of the next 2 loops, turn and work 4 d c over the 6 ch, then 3 ch into 2nd braid, 1 d c, 6 ch, 1 d c into next 2 loops, turn, 4 d c over the 6 ch, 3 ch to 1st braid.

A PLEATED NET DESIGN.

Braid Appliqué
on Net.

Continue in this way till the corner is reached, then from the 1 d c in top braid carry 8 ch to lower braid, miss 1 loop, then work 4 d c in the 8 ch, from the 4th d c work 4 ch back to lower braid, miss 2 loops and join with d c, work 4 d c over this 4 ch, 1 d c to middle of 8 ch, 4 ch back again to lower braid, miss 2 loops and return with 4 d c to centre of 8 ch, 3 ch to top braid and continue as before. When the next corner is required work in same way as just directed, but this time making the

The pleated net should then be tacked to the depth of the middle part and the insertion placed in position and edges sewn. Afterwards place upon plain net and sew the other side of the insertion.

A Leaf Spray
for Appliqué.

This suggestion could be used with or without the crochet. If the latter is used it is worked as the braid is twisted in. In this case, begin a few loops from the end of the braid: 1 d c into each of 3 loops, 2 ch between

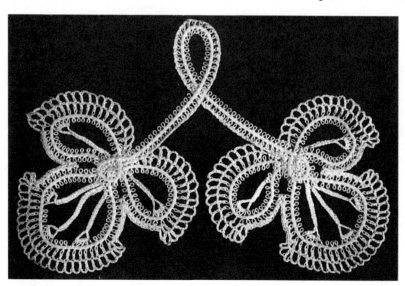

A LEAF SPRAY FOR APPLIQUÉ.

spray of 3 bars join to upper instead of lower braid. When the loops of braid are reached, curl the upper braid to size of oval required and work the stitches going into upper braid through double loops at the joins to hold firmly.

For the outer edge work 1 d c into every loop with 2 ch between. At corners miss 3 loops. Round the edge of the ovals work 2 tr into each loop with 2 ch between. Have the same number each side.

each 5 ch, 1 tr into the next 15 loops, 2 ch between each, 4 ch, 1 d c in same loop as last treble, 1 d c in next 8 loops, 2 ch between each, miss 12 loops and bend round for middle leaf, next 8 loops 1 d c 2 ch between each 4 ch, 1 tr in same loop as last d c, then 1 tr in each of the next 22 loops, with 2 ch between each, 8 d c, miss 12 loops and work 3rd leaf same as first. Sew these in position without wrapping more than possible, then curl round the braid and catch down to form a little finish.

For the outer edge work d c 2 d c into each 2 ch space, 5 ch 1 tr into each tr of previous row, with 3 ch between each.

For veins work a chain from one of the top loops to one of the bottom loops of the leaf, d c along 3 loops, work 5 ch and join into the 5 ch of bar, work over the remaining ch with d c's.

A POINT WITH LACE BRAID.

For the stem, from leaf work about 65 d c into loops, where stem twists catch with needle and cotton, and proceed with second set of leaves in same way as the first.

Attractive Corners.

In the two corners worked with a fine Feather-stitched Braid, on pages 77 and 78, the work is the same, but the braid is arranged somewhat differently.

For this use Feather-stitched Braid of the finest quality, and No. 50 crochet cotton. For the motif cut off a length of 3½ inches of

the braid, turn in the ends neatly and secure with a few stitches, then cut a length of 2½ inches and form the cross, the triangle is 3¾ inches of the braid formed into the angle in the centre. Sew all securely together, commencing at the edge of the left arm of the cross, work a row of d c into the openwork on the braid and continue around the top down to the opposite point, 15 ch to cross the end of the arm, 1 d c into the corner of the underside, make five 5 ch loops fastened with d c into the spaces on this side, finish the side with d c into each space, work a corresponding

A NOVEL CORNER ARRANGEMENT.

Braid Appliqué on Net.

number of d c into the next side of the triangle, then the 5 ch loops down to the end of this strip, cross over the end with 15 ch and work all the edges in the same way, after fastening the 15 ch over the end of the left arm, turn and put * 4 tr, 4 long tr, 4 triple tr, 4 long tr, 4 tr, then into each 5 ch loop put 2 d c 4 ch 2 d c, omitting the picot in the 2 loops at the end of each angle, * repeat all round.

3rd Row.—* 3 ch, 1 tr 1 ch into the space between the trs around the end, make a length of chs sufficient to reach the corner of the triangle and repeat from *.

4th Row.—2 tr over every 1 ch between the trs, work d c closely over the ch bars with a 5 ch picot after every 5th d c.

The Corner Design.

Cut off the length of braid required and form the angles for the corners. These are sewn into shape.

For the inner side, 2 d c into 2 spaces on the edge of the braid, * 4 ch, miss 2 spaces, 2 d c into next 2, * repeat all round.

2nd Row.—Into every 2nd loop put 2 tr, 5 ch between, omit the chs in the corners.

For the lower side of the top strip of braid, work the 1st row as at the other side.

2nd Row.—Commencing at a corner loop in the preceding row, with 2 d c into it, 5 ch 1 d c into each of the next 2 loops, 3 ch 2 tr into next, 3 ch 2 long tr into next, 3 ch, 2 long tr into next, 3 ch 2 tr into next, 3 ch 2 d c into next * repeat.

Work the lower strip of braid with the 1st row at each side as in the upper.

2nd Row on the Inner Side.—Fasten the thread in the first corner loop with a d c, 5 ch 1 d c into next loop, * pass over 3 loops, 15 ch 1 d c into next, 5 ch 1 d c into each of next 3 loops, * repeat.

3rd Row.—1 d c into the top of the corner loop, * 10 ch 1 d c over the centre of the 15 ch, 6 ch 1 d c beside the last d c, 10 ch 1 d c into next loop, 5 ch 1 d c into each of next 2 loops, * repeat.

4th Row.—1 d c into the picot, 10 ch, fasten this with a d c to the corner of the first strip into the second of the 2 d c, turn back on the chs and put 12 d c over them, * 10 ch 1 d c into next loop, 5 ch 1 d c into next, 10 ch 1 d c into next picot, 6 ch 1 d c into same picot, * repeat, catching in with every picot the 3 ch between the long trs on the first strip of braid, so connecting the strips.

The 2nd, 3rd, and 4th rows at the outer edge are worked like those at the opposite side, but at each side of a corner put 4 loops in the group.

5th Row.—Into each 5 ch loop put 3 long trs into each picot 1 long tr, 5 ch, 1 long tr, 5 ch, 1 triple tr, 5 ch, 1 triple tr, 5 ch, 1 long tr, 5 ch, 1 long tr. At each side of a corner there are 2 loops together, into each of these put the 3 long trs, turn and put 3 loops of 5 ch each, fastened between the trs with a d c, turn, 1 ch 1 d c into 1st loop, 5 ch 1 d c into each of the others, 1 ch 1 d c into the top of the tr, then put the long trs and chs into both corner picots.

The motif and lace are appliquéd on the net by sewing the net to the braid along both edges on the wrong side.

A Point with Lace Braid.

This shows a light and pretty idea for a corner. Here two kinds of braid are used, and very little stitchery is required. The little loops of braid are first sewn to the edge of the net and afterwards it is made quite neat by the straight band of braid sewn over.

INSERTION WITH DIAMOND DESIGN IN MOSAIC FILET LACE.

See the directions on page 103.

Darned Huckaback.

Darned Huckaback is always in good taste for towels. The work is easy to do and inexpensive, and a very small expenditure of labour suffices to produce, from 'a piece of huckaback and a few skeins of thread, not only towels but many other articles that call for ornamentation that will stand hard wear.

Huckaback can be had in various qualities; some of it is of "Old Bleach" linen, and beautifully soft to work upon, creamy in tint and rather coarse in texture; that known as Union, and which is a mixture of linen and cotton, is a purer white, a finer mesh, and for certain patterns answers sufficiently well.

You will see here 4 different patterns for darning on huckaback, and when you realize that Fig. 2 is a detail of the towel design shown in Fig. 1, you will understand how the effect varies according to the texture of the background material.

The towel being of rather closely woven huckaback, was worked with longer stitches than those used on the small detail. Usually every one of the raised threads that are the distinguishing feature in huckaback weaving, is picked up by the needle following the outlines of the pattern chosen: in the towel-end, for a bold effect, every alternate one only of these threads was lifted.

The threads to be used are lustrines such as Ardern's Star Sylko, or Vicar's "Brillianté," which can be obtained in many pretty shades. These threads usually come in 3 sizes, fine, medium and coarse, suited for fine, medium and coarse "huck" respectively. For washing articles, boiling dyes should

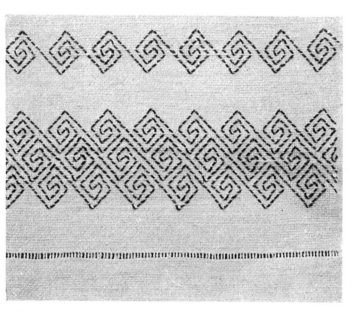

Fig. 1. A TOWEL IN GREEK FRET DESIGN.

be selected, for other goods, any preferred colour scheme can be followed.

In the towel in Fig. 1, the threads are all taken up in diagonal succession, not right up and down the fabric. For the longest lines of this Greek Fret design raise 10 threads in succession, working upwards and from right to left; pick up 4, passing down again as if tracing an inverted letter V; 3 threads still downwards

80

but from left
to right;
2 upwards,
forming a
small V; 2
downwards,
inside that V
as it were; 3
up, follow-
ing the outer
left hand
slope and
towards the
right; 3
downwards
to the right,
inside the
first line of
10 stitches;
3 down and

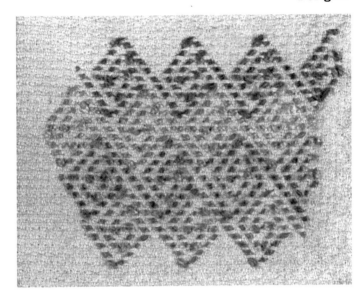

Fig. 2. THIS SHOWS THE DETAIL OF THE TOWEL.

to the left; then, starting 1 loop lower
still, begin again with a set of 10 loops
lifted. Continue thus all across the
work. The towel is worked in the
same way, but the darning is under
every alternate loop, thus enlarging
the pattern.

If other rows are needed to form a
wide band or all-over design, these
are easily arranged, as the illustrations show, and dovetail exactly in
with one another and with the first
row worked.

The towel edge is embroidered with
scarlet; for
the detail
deep yellow,
pale green,
bright blue
and cop-
pery orange
threads were
selected.

Figure 3 is a
little design
that was
worked in
orange and
red; any pre-
ferred mix-
ture could be
made use of,
but the

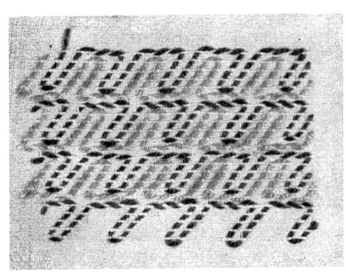

Fig 4. A PATTERN IN BOLD VANDYKES.

Darned Huckaback.

Fig. 3. A ZIG-ZAG PATTERN.

effect will be so different, according to the tints used, as to surprise those unfamiliar with the work. In suitable colours this pattern is well adapted for small articles.

The straight, orange threads are laid first, and are in plain darning carried along every alternate row of loops on the huckaback, and passing under every one of these loops.

The red lines are in zig-zags and managed thus : raise 4 loops side by side just below a yellow line, bring the thread up and to the right, under the loop where is also a yellow strand; still up and to the right and the nearest free loop ; under 3 more loops parallel and going

towards the left, down and under a loop where is a yellow strand, in the same direction and lift the loop next to the left of the 4 first loops raised ; this is the first loop of the next set of 4 that begins the repeat of the pattern. Continue this in every row, but alternate the zig-zags so as to leave no free and unraised loops.

Figure 4 is also in bold vandykes, but here no 2 threads pass through the same loop. Scarlet and pale green were the tints used and the same outline was followed by each thread, only the stitches were so set that those of one row exactly alternated with and fitted in with those of the next. Four strands were raised for the longest straight stitch, 4 more upward and slanting to the right, 4 down again side by side with this first slant and so on all along. This for the scarlet

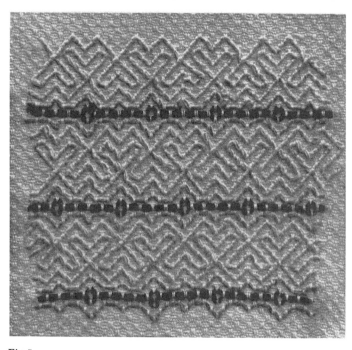

Fig. 5. A BROCADED EFFECT.

rows; in the green, the 4 threads raised came at the top and the slopes pointed downwards and to the left.

Figure 5 is a sample of more elaborate stitchery that gives somewhat the effect of brocade. Blue and green and blue and pink were employed for the interlacings of the stripes, with straighter lines of black, bordered with dull gold. Black is exceedingly effective, but must only be used sparingly. In this pattern the black thread must be finer than the coloured, as a double line of it runs through the same sets of loops. Five straight stitches are followed by one raised just above the line (raised by one black strand) and another raised just below the line and for which the 2nd black strand only is employed. The dull gold thread follows the outline of the black, but is raised to one strand beyond the centre loop of the 5 straight black stitches; thus vandyking it a little. Between the rows of black and gold are the heart-shaped lines that give one into the other. Seven strands or

loops are raised in succession for the longest lines, and the thread passes twice through the 4th of these after completing half the width of the row that it is working. It should be noticed that the bands of pattern are arranged to set alternately, as this looks far better, especially on account of the black rows, than if they were placed exactly one under the other.

Other patterns, easy and elaborate, can be contrived by any worker who has once successfully managed one design.

As regards its uses, Huckaback darning is adapted for use on towels, cushion-covers, aprons, work-bags, nightdress cases and many other articles. Marking can be effected in this manner and with good effect.

Two further cautions alone are necessary: use a blunt needle (a rug needle) and do not let any stitches be seen on the wrong side of the work. Begin and fasten off invisibly under the stitches that are over the right side of the huckaback.

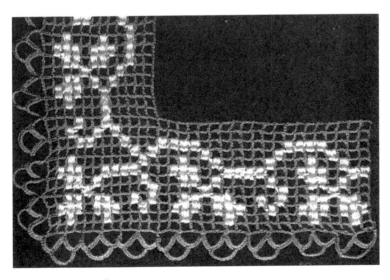

A border for a Tablecloth, made by darning filet crochet, open mesh.
The edge is finished with loops and double crochet.

Finishing the Edges of Cushions.

We have all made cushions, and we have all finished them off in the ordinary way, with a frill or a cord, and probably we have wished we knew of some other way we could finish them for a change. There are quite a lot of other ways. A few are shown and described here, and as you will easily see, they can all be

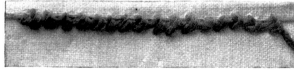

A very simple stitch in embroidery silk.

enlarged and improved upon, and you will doubtless think of a good many more things that you can do with the edges of your cushion covers.

First of all, and probably one of the most beautiful, is the cushion cover with the fringed ends shown. The sides are finished with a little fancy stitching that completely covers the seams, and the ends are fringed by unravelling the weft of the linen

An edge of this kind makes a good finish.

and knotting the warp. This makes a beautiful setting for the handsome piece of embroidery. A working detail, showing how to start the fringe, is shown, and full directions as to how to make fringes appear on another page in this volume. This is quite one of the simplest of fringes, and yet most effective.

Some very attractive finishings may be obtained by the use of embroidery stitches, using several strands of embroidery silk, and employing quite simple stitchery. The three examples shown would be quite easy to work, and the addition of a tassel at the corner is in good taste. These are all shown with the edges opened flat, that it may be more easily seen how

This quite hides the seam, and is most effective.

84

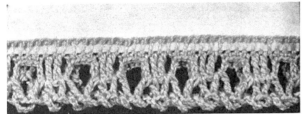

A crochet finish with the two edges laced together.

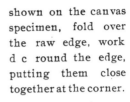

shown on the canvas specimen, fold over the raw edge, work d c round the edge, putting them close together at the corner.

2nd Row.—* 2 tr

they are w o r k e d. T h e s e stitches of course quite cover the seams.

Again, crochet can be success-fully employed for this purpose. In the crochet specimens two patterns are illustrated, each of which is shown opened flat and also closed. W h e r e a cushion cover is of canvas, a crocheted edge of the same colour as the work on the cushion is most suitable. A

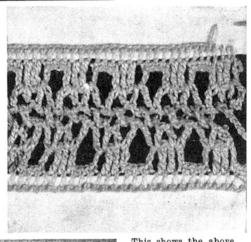

This shows the above finish with the two edges opened flat.

into d c, 2 ch, miss 1 d c. Repeat from *. No d c's are to be missed at the corners. When the crochet is finished, l a c e t h e edges together.

A great advantage of this simple lacing is that it can easily be

A good edge for a Canvas Cushion Cover.

little finish is crocheted on all the sides, and the crochet edges are t h e n laced together either with very fine cord or a length of chain.

To make the e d g e

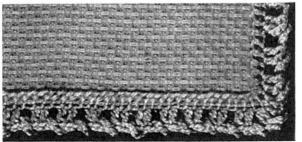

A cover of the design above with the edges laced.

Finishing the Edges of Cushions.

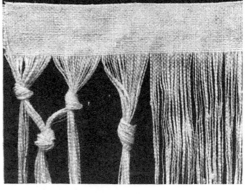

Commencing the Fringe for the design below.

undone, and the cushion slipped out for the cover to be laundered, no further fastening being necessary.

The other crochet edging is commenced by turning in the edge and working buttonhole stitch all round, making the work closer at the corners.

1st Row.—* 1 d c in each of first 4 buttonhole stitches, 4 ch, 1 long tr in each of 2 next stitches, 4 ch. Repeat from *.

2nd Row.—Into 1st space made by long tr and ch of previous row, put * 1 long tr, 3 ch, 1 tr, miss the next space, and into the next put 1 tr, 3 ch, 1 long tr. Repeat from *. Then lace the edges together.

The fancy edge on the inner side is made by catching each buttonholed thread and working into each stitch like one side of ordinary feather-stitching.

A Handsome Cushion. The side seams are hidden by the embroidery stitching, and the ends are fringed.

Rhodes Embroidery.

This work is so called because it is a revival of some old Greek work, done by the peasants of Rhodes Island, of which some very beautiful specimens may be seen in the Victoria and Albert

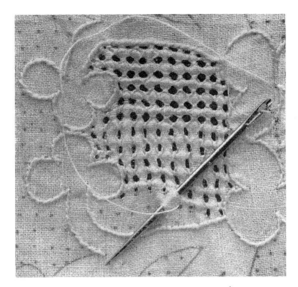

SHOWING THE WORK BEING DONE.

Museum. In this work, however, the effect is produced by the threads being drawn out, but no difficulty caused by the drawing of threads presents itself to the modern worker of Rhodes Embroidery. The threads are simply forced apart with a very coarse needle, and then bound with a strong linen thread.

Materials Required.

The requisites necessary for this work are the design, which can be obtained ready stamped on the material for working, an embroidery needle for outlining the design, embroidery cotton, a "Rhodes" needle, for punching the holes and binding the threads, and

Fig. 1.

A	1	2	3	4	5	6	A
B	7	8	9	10	11	12	B
C	13	14	15	16	17	18	C

Fig. 2.

	C	B	A	
D	13	7	1	D
E	14	8	2	E
	15	9	3	
	16	10	4	
	17	11	5	
	18	12	6	
	C	B	A	

With "Rhodes" Needle under and out at 7.

INTO	1	OUT AT	7	
,,	1	,,	8	
,,	2	,,	8	
,,	2	,,	9	AA
,,	3	,,	9	
,,	3	,,	10	
,,	4	,,	10	
,,	4	,,	11	BB
,,	5	,,	11	
,,	5	,,	12	
,,	6	,,	12	
,,	6	,,	18	
,,	12	,,	18	
,,	12	,,	17	
	AND	SO	ON	

Rhodes Embroidery.

some strong linen thread for this part of the work.

Method of Working.

The first step is to outline the design, and obviously

A DESIGN FOR A TEA COSY IN RHODES EMBROIDERY.

Following these instructions with the diagram, it will be seen that the method is one stitch on the perpendicular and onestitch

the larger the design is, the less space there is to be taken up by the openwork in the background. This outlining is done with the embroidery cotton, and is a perfectly simple matter.

Now for the openwork, tie an end of linen thread into the eye of a "Rhodes" needle, and bring it from the wrong, through the right side of the work at the 1st dot in the 2nd row—or dot 7 on the diagram; push it through to the wrong side on the dot immediately above (dot 1). Bring it up at the 2nd dot of the 2nd row (dot 8). Then push it down again at the 2nd dot of the 1st row (dot 2) and up on the 3rd dot of the 2nd row (dot 9).

on the diagonal, the first of these ties the fabric threads, the second brings the needle in position for the next stitch. When the end of a row of dots is reached, start the row below. After tying the threads at dot 12, the needle put in at dot 6 is brought out at dot 18, and is thus in position for the next stitch. It is then put in at 12 and out at 18, again tying the threads, then in at 12 and out at 17, and so on.

When all is worked in this manner from A A to C C, reverse the material as in Fig. 2, and repeat the instructions working from D E to D E.

There is really not the slightest difficulty about this work, merely a

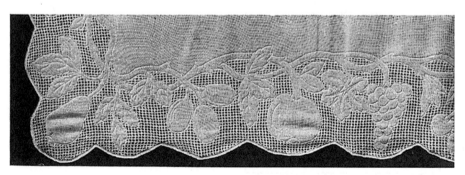

RHODES EMBROIDERY AS A BORDER.

AN EXCEEDINGLY HANDSOME DESIGN
IN RHODES EMBROIDERY.

little care being required to see that while the stitches are pulled firmly, they are not drawn so as to pucker the material. Cluny lace makes an excellent finish for this kind of work, which is sometimes called Punched Embroidery.

Where to Get Materials.

All the requisites for this work can be obtained from the Broderie Russe Co., 289, Regent St., London, W.

A ROUND FIVE O'CLOCK TEA CLOTH
IN RHODES EMBROIDERY.

They are the sole Patentees for this embroidery, and all the illustrations on these pages are their copyright, and can be obtained from them. They have other beautiful designs traced on a large number of articles, including d'oilies, tray cloths, tea cloths cosies, night dress cases, chair backs, etc., and they will commence a piece of work if required. No one need be afraid to attempt this embroidery, and quite a small square can be purchased to experiment on. Rhodes embroidery is so fascinating to do, however, that the worker will soon want to start something more ambi-

tious. It would be advisable for beginners not to start with a circle or curved piece of material, something having a squared edge would be easier as a commencement, until proficiency is attained.

The Mending Basket.

Mending and altering are two branches of the great art of Needle-craft which no woman can afford to despise in these days of ready-made frocks and shop-bought costumes. Turnings may be insufficient, buttons sewn on with too scant stitches, hooks and eyes trembing to fall off, but these deficiencies very easily can be put to rights. A shop-bought costume that does not fit, however, is not cheap at any price. Learn, therefore, how to make alterations in the most commonsense and practical fashion, and take preventive measures, before the garment is worn for the first time, to overcome the little deficiencies that we may expect to discover in the "ready-mades."

**Tools for the Practical
Needlewoman.**

Chief among the aids for the practical needlewoman, taking first rank among her valuable assistants, comes the sewing-machine. For hard wear and every-day use machine-stitching is generally much neater and stronger than hand sewing, and the pace, of course, is far quicker. Her sewing-machine is a good friend to the busy woman who has most need to practise the art of preventive mending, for strength and speed are two of her chief demands.

It pays to understand one's sewing-machine, and to treat it with tender

care. Rough usage, or careless handling, through ignorance of the rightful functions of the different delicate pieces, may lead to dire disaster. A handbook of instructions is always given when the machine is purchased ; cherish this book, for if it is mislaid you are at sea without your chart. The inexperienced girl who makes her early attempt to fathom the mysteries of the sewing-machine will find that a little personal instruction (which may be had at the depôt of her own make of machine) will be more helpful than an hour spent in trying to solve intricate problems by the aid of the printed page. Later on, however, the printed directions will read lucidly enough when her mind is conversant with the everyday workings of the machine, and an intelligent glance at her useful little handbook will disclose to her the cause and the remedy of the defective action.

Keep the machine scrupulously clean and thoroughly well oiled. To do this is again to recognise the wisdom of preventive measures. An un-oiled, dirty machine will always cause trouble in working, for when the parts do not run smoothly, dropped and uneven stitches are a frequent embarrassment.

Oil in every part, and open and turn back so that when the oil has soaked through, the clogged dirt may be carefully cleaned away.

A capacious mending basket is a necessity for the practical worker, and it is all the more convenient if it stands upon legs, table height, and can be carried about to be stationed just within comfortable reach of the mender's right hand.

Keep always some tailor's canvas for use as stiffening, buckram for millinery, white leno and fine black lining, rolls of old linen and flannel for patching, stray pieces of lace, and left-over lengths of embroidery or insertions. Roll up all oddments in soft, clean muslin with tape or label attached, on which is written a list of the trifles to be found within your treasury.

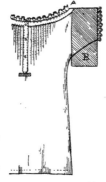

DIAGRAM SHOWING HOW TO MEND A CHEMISE SLEEVE-

If you frequently find your tape measure mislaid, try this plan, and thus prevent the long searching that interrupts your sewing. Cut as long a piece off your tape as will stretch from end to end of your machine, and paste it along the front edge of the stand. It thus will be *always* at hand when required, and will serve at any rate for all the shorter measurements required.

It is a good plan to assemble your hooks and eyes on safety pins. Slip the opened pin through the separate hooks and eyes, then when they are all securely dangling, firmly close your safety pin, and they are ready for use when needed and will not get

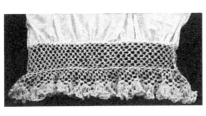

A SIMPLE WAY TO RENOVATE KNICKERS WHEN THE FRILLS HAVE WORN OUT.

tangled and twisted together as so often happens if they are kept in a box.

Keep odd buttons in glass bottles. No more hunting in the dark and dust ! You can see the button for which you are searching, and by shaking the bottle can bring it near to the top, where it can be easily reached. Bone or pearl buttons for underwear, or any others that are not affected by exposure, may be securely fixed upon a hairpin. Straighten out one of the long hairpins, bend back one end about a quarter or half an inch, run the point through the holes, and when your buttons are neatly crowded together turn up the other end to hold them securely.

Preventive Mending.

We have heard that in China it is the custom to pay the family doctor to keep his patients in good health rather than to call him in only after illness has laid the sufferer low. Many of us applaud this system, but have neither the opportunity nor, perhaps, the courage, to defy conventions in our own country.

But why not pursue the same wise course in dealing with household mending ? It works admirably.

Take the proverbial stitch that "saves nine" in very good time, even before there is any apparent need for it, and you'll find it will work miracles.

Stockings, for instance. The toes

THE JOY OF THE HOUSEWIFE WHEN SHE EXAMINES THE LAUNDRY HAMPER!

and heels of children's stockings may be neatly darned before they are worn for the first time, for this purpose using crochet silk or mercerised thread, which is less bulky and clumsy than wool. Insist on frequent change of hosiery and forbid the wearing of any stocking that shows even the tiniest hole. To prevent those long running ladders which are almost impossible to mend, sew a band of silk or cotton, or a border cut from an old stocking, round each hem of the new pair. Hose supporters (chief cause of these destructive ladders) will seldom cut through this double band. Or another excellent plan may be adopted. Take a round brass ring and d c closely over it to make a soft, firm covering. Sew this firmly into position upon the stocking top with neat, strong stitches, and always insert the clip of the suspender within this ring. You will thus make it impossible for the tension to strain the stocking beyond the area enclosed by the ring.

In the knees of children's stockings small shields may be placed, pieces cut from other stockings and fastened in so neatly that they are quite inconspicuous and not at all uncomfortable.

To strengthen the heel and underpart of the foot when making men's or boy's stockings, knit stout mercerised cotton along with the wool. This does not make it so clumsy as 2 strands of wool, yet it adds considerably to the wearing quality of the stocking.

The "ready-mades," whether visiting frocks, walking suits, or underwear, as was hinted in a previous paragraph, cry out loudly for preventive mending. For instance, sleeves should be stitched in by machine, for on ready-made clothes the machine stitching is not always carefully done, and a weak place in the sleeve seam will quickly give way under strain and start an ugly tear.

Embroidery with scalloped or pointed edging should be machined strongly all round the extreme edges, the machine needle patiently following the circuitous course of the pattern. This will double the life of embroided lace, preventing frayed untidiness and breaks, gaps and tears.

CASH'S INSERTIONS ARE ADMIRABLE FOR MENDING TRAY-CLOTHS.

To prevent an embroidery flounce from ragging out before the petticoat itself is any the worse for wear, neatly hem the edge as soon as it threatens to fray or gets torn by an accidental mis-step, and add a bordering of Valenciennes or fine Torchon lace.

Buttons should receive careful attention when any ready-made garment is bought. The trimness of effect and the general prettiness of coat or costume may be entirely spoilt if one of a set of distinctive buttons is allowed to drop off and get lost.

Therefore sew on all buttons at the time of your purchase. Stitch carefully with a strong thread; when you have sewn through and through the button half a dozen times, wind your thread round and round the strands which hold the button, between the button and the cloth, making a sort of shank. Treat boot and shoe buttons in the

AN ECONOMICAL TRAY-CLOTH
MADE FROM SCRAPS.

MACHINE-MADE NET SQUARES
FOR MENDING TEA CLOTHS.

same way.

It is wise to strengthen bedlinen with broad tape laid on at the corners, inconspicuously stitched into position, so that an added firmness is given to the sheets where the clothes-pegs might do most damage.

Tablecloths are wonderfully strengthened if tape is sewn all down the long sides. This is the part that goes first.

Look closely into the wool-worked buttonholing at your blanket ends. You may, with advantage, stitch fresh buttonhole edgings that will keep the neat turn-over, when the blanket is in use, for a longer time than if the shop-bought edging were left to suffice.

Mending a Child's Chemise.

Half an hour spent weekly in preventive mending will often save hours of darning and patching later. At the

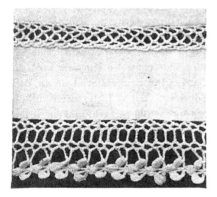

A NARROW CROCHET INSERTION IS USEFUL
IN REPAIRING TORN HEMSTITCHING.

same time, there will always be holes and tears, and it is well to learn the best methods of repairing the various damages.

As children's clothes quickly and so often require mending, shall we consider the repairing of a little girl's chemise? These directions are suitable for a chemise with a round band. The first thing to happen will most likely be its return from the

A CHILD'S PETTICOAT MADE FROM DONE-WITH STOCKING LEGS.

wash with a button missing. Now don't hastily catch one on, or you will have the same business to do next week. First be sure that your button is the right size for your button hole. One too large would be obviously useless, one too small will come unfastened and cause discomfort. The plain linen buttons are preferable, those with holes cut the cotton and cause the threads to come undone. Sew on firmly, stemming, i.e., twist the cotton several times round the button, and cast off securely on the back.

The next trouble will probably be a slit down the front from the opening; this will possibly be very slight, but a darn is not a sufficient form of strengthening. Place a piece of wide tape across the slit, on the wrong side of the garment, and sew round securely. Some find a piece of tape on both sides acts well for hard wear, but this would be too clumsy for light garments.

A chemise that is in otherwise good condition may perhaps become slightly frayed at the bottom. This is easily made perfect by cutting off the bottom hem, turning up and machining another. Do not tear off this hem, but cut it off, as the threads round the bottom of the chemise do not always run evenly.

The sleeve is a part that constantly comes to grief with growing girls. Physical drill, hockey, etc., while giving good exercise to the arms, also causes much wear on the parts of the chemise round the shoulder. Patching here is very unsatisfactory, for if you patch one side one week the other will need it the next, and the top the next after, making a very unsightly and uncomfortable garment. The remedy for this is to put in an entirely new sleeve, which is very easily done.

Take an oblong piece of material, fold to form a square, place the fold over the shoulder part of sleeve, having first unpicked the neck band over the shoulder. One end of square goes into the band. (A in diagram). This may be cut out a little if necessary; the other side of the square comes to the arm-hole of sleeve. Pin new material on to the old sleeve, cut out the curve under arm by the old pattern, make a seam and fell on that curve to correspond with the side of chemise. (B in diagram). Sew round the right side of the patch, being particular that the seam and fell of the new sleeve come exactly on the seam and fell of

94

the chemise. Now turn the chemise inside out and cut out the old sleeve, leaving enough material to turn in and make a neat hem all round. Sew on the part of the band that was unpicked, hem the arm-hole.

Possibly by this time the neck band is wearing. Never patch a band, it is lumpy and looks most ugly. This should be taken off and a new band put on. The band is simply a long narrow strip of calico. Measure the length by the old one, halve and quarter this band, see that the half comes to the middle of the back gathers and the quarters on the shoulders ; pin these points while you tack the band, it can then be machined. Work a buttonhole, put on a button and finish with trimming. If the trimming on the original band was good it should bear using again ; if it is worn, put on some narrow Cash's Frilling or crocheted edging.

Often it happens that the top back of the chemise is much worn ; in this case a neat patch might be put in while the band is off. Press out the old gathers before placing the patch ; remember to gather the back when the patch has been completed before replacing the band. If the two new sleeves are put in at the same time the chemise will take an entirely new lease of life.

A Simple Knicker Frill.

Unfortunately, by far the larger part of our mending, nowadays, is due to the modern laundry. Where our mothers could keep their under-clothing in good condition for years, ours is torn to shreds, and some of it comes home ragged and tattered most weeks from the average laundry. Knicker frills go very quickly, and often need replacing.

Here is a simple way to renovate them. Crochet a band of insertion, and add a crochet frill; gather the leg of the knicker, and whip it to one edge of the band of insertion. You will find this will wear well, and look better than patched embroidery.

Mending Table Linen.

The damage here is chiefly of two sorts ; thin places where the laundry has removed stains—always without chemicals of course !—and perhaps a little hole in the middle, and clean knife cuts. The latter should be darned at once, whether it crumples the cloth or not, while other darns are usually left till the cloth is ready for the wash.

To darn a cut, first catch its edges lightly together with coloured cotton, so that it lies quite flat and closed. Then thread a crewel needle with medium course linen thread for a tablecloth, or with fine thread for a fine d'oily. The shape of the darn will be a parallelogram, the sides slanting according to the direction of the cut, but the stitches always exactly in line with the selvedge of the material. When the darn is completed to about half-an-inch beyond each end of the cut that is sufficient, and you have then only to remove the coloured cotton.

A round hole or thin place is darned just as a stocking-hole, but you must be more careful than ever that the crossing threads do not go through the material, but only pick up the first darning threads, and see that you *do* pick up the threads entirely without splitting them.

When table-cloths get worn or frayed, or in any way damaged at the edges, it may be possible to mend and darn and even patch the edges for a little while; but the most satisfactory way in the end is to cut the edges right off and turn down a hem. The cloth will then take on a new lease of life.

Tray-cloths.

Speaking of the ravages of the laundry, reminds me of the way tray-cloths and fancy tea-cloths get torn if there is any drawn-thread work or hem-stitching. Most housewives have had occasion to mourn damages such as the one illustrated on page 92. Now a quick way to repair hemstitching or narrow drawn-thread work, when it runs all round the cloth, is to put some of Cash's insertion over the damaged line, carrying it right out to the edge of the cloth, since it is a little difficult to make neat at the corners; featherstitch down each side of the insertion. Or a narrow insertion can be crocheted. The specimen shown is simply loops of 5 ch, each row caught into the row below. This does well to go with a firm material.

When fancy corners get torn out, a square of fine crocheted filet mesh can be let in, and the material cut away to fit. If the cloth is too thin to take anything as strong as crochet, a piece of darned net let in will often look well, and give the cloth a new lease of life. Also, you can get from Messrs. S. Peach & Co., The Looms, Nottingham, small squares in fine machine-made net, that are not so heavy as crochet for letting into a cloth that is partly worn. And these are quite inexpensive; they are about 5 inches square. (See illustration on page 93).

"Hedge-tear" in a Dress.

This is unfortunately as common as it is annoying, and not so very easy to repair either. First of all, if the dress be lined, you must get a hem or seam open somewhere in order to work on the wrong side. Then catch the edges of the tear together, keeping them very flat, and if it be large or awkward to hold, or very dark in colour, tack the whole smoothly on to a stiff piece of white card. Now choose your darning thread and needle. For a woollen dress there is nothing less conspicuous than ravellings of the material itself, but failing this the silk or wool must be matched very carefully.

Use as fine a needle as is practicable. Start darning from half-an-inch to an inch beyond one end of the tear and work backward and forward across it, going on each side half-an-inch beyond the frayed portion. However much frayed the tear may be, do not cut away the roughness, but stroke it flat with the needle, and be very careful to weave the darning strand neatly and securely through it. Work right to the end of one slit, and then start from the further end of the other slit, so that the 2 sets of darning meet and cross at the angle, thus giving additional strength just where it is most needed. The darning completed, you can then remove the tacking stitches and the card, and with a warm iron press the place firmly on the wrong side. If in tearing, the material has been dragged very much out of shape so that now it is darned it does not lie flat, put a damp cloth over it, and iron through that till the cloth is dry. Then repeat the process, if necessary, so long as it seems to be doing any good at all. It is wise first to try on the back of a hem or seam whether the material will stand this without

changing colour or cockling. Then
you have simply to replace your hem
or seam, and wear your dress, deter-
mined to believe that everyone else
does not know exactly where to look
for that darn.

Those Stocking Legs!

Even when the feet of stockings
seem to be too far gone to be of any
use, it is possible to turn them to
practical use if the legs are all right.
The little petticoat illustrated on page
94 illustrates this.

Cut off the worn portion. Then cut
the stocking down the back seam.
When the pieces are spread out flat,
it will be seen that they are gore-
shaped, being wide at the top of the
stocking, and narrowing as the heel
is approached. By joining a
number
of "legs"
together,
the wide
part gives
the neces-
sary flare
at the
bottom of
the petti-
coat, and
the nar-
row part
goes into
the waist-
band.
Bind the
bottom
with some
crimson
braid, and
put the

upper part on a waistband, and you
will have a warm petticoat that will
be a boon to any poor child.

Using up the Pieces.

One often has nice pieces of linen
or other material left over, when making, that might be turned to good
account. The tray-cloth, shown on
page 93, was made from 2 pieces of
plain tea-cloth linen that were over
after some aprons had been cut out.
The material is beautifully serviceable,
but too stout to hem; so each piece
was bound round with some narrow
strips of nainsook—likewise cast aside
for the piece-bag. These binding
strips were feather-stitched round.

A piece of simple Irish insertion
took very little time to crochet,
and used
only a
small
amount
of cotton.
Ardern's
No. 24
was used,
as the
coarser
thread
went
better
than a
finer one
with the
stout
material.
The whole
was edged
with some
crochet.

A PRETTY ARRANGEMENT OF
TENERIFFE WHEELS.

No directions can be
supplied for this.

Princess Braid Appliqué.

This is a very simple form of lace to make, and yet, when done, looks wonderfully effective. The design shown, being arranged in the form of a square, would be most suitable for the corner of a square collar, but it would be a perfectly simple matter to arrange the same design on an entirely different shaped foundation, and use it for a collar of any other shape, or for any other purpose desired.

The only materials required for this pretty work are some fine Brussels net, lace braid, some crochet cotton and fine lace thread. A row of pearl edging is often sewn round the edge of a collar to finish it off. This edging can be bought at any fancy work depôt.

The sprays are formed of lobes of braid, with braid of a larger kind for the leaves, and the stems are worked in twist stitch with Ardern's No. 24 Lustrous Crochet Cotton.

First draw the design on paper, tack a piece of Brussels net over the paper, then apply the braid, and sew round with neat, even stitches, using very fine thread for the purpose.

It will easily be seen that by varying the arrangement of the braid, and even the braid itself, a variety of different designs can be obtained. For instance, pretty flowers are made by using four or five loops of the plain lace braid (the kind used for the inside straight border of the design here illustrated), and working in the centre, where the loops meet, a group of French knots. Then too, leaflets, and other small parts of designs, are sometimes worked in darning.

As mentioned above, a pearl edging whipped along the edge, makes a pretty finish for a collar, handkerchief border, or length of lace.

A CORNER IN PRINCESS BRAID APPLIQUÉ.

98

How Needlework Reveals Our Aims.

By the Editor.

At first glance it may seem strange — if one has not thought about the matter—to say that our needlework will, to some extent, reveal our aims in life. Yet it is true ; and whether we know it or not, our hand-work, and the way we do it, gives a wonderfully accurate indication of some of our chief characteristics, be they good or bad. More than this, the style of needlework that we do as a recreation, in our spare time, will to a very large extent help to mould our taste and influence us in a way we little imagine.

Speaking broadly, all needlework, whether it be plain or fancy stitchery, crochet or knitting, can be placed under one or two heads : good art and bad art. Of course there are many grades, and a multiplicity of degrees of excellence ; but in the main it is not at all difficult to decide to which category a piece of work belongs ; as a rule it falls easily into its proper division : there is no halfway house.

Is the work exactly what it pretends to be ? Does it serve some definite purpose ? Is it a type of work suited to the purpose for which it is to be used ? Is it executed as well as the worker knows how ? Is it done thoroughly ? Is it done in such a way that it will wear well, and last long by reason of its careful workmanship ? If so, the probability is that it will be good art.

On the other hand : Is the work a base, flimsy imitation of some superior form of the craft ? Is it executed with the definite intention of deceiving the eye ? Is it shoddy work, or a sham ? Is it carelessly done, with no attention to finish ? Is it unsuited to the purpose for which it is to be used ? Is it all surface show, with no body in it that will stand legitimate wear ? Is it the type of work that demands neither thought nor mechanical skill from the worker ? Then there is no question but that it will be bad art.

Consider a concrete case and you will see more clearly what I mean. I saw a girl doing a piece of so-called embroidery the other day—wild roses on white satin it purported to be. But when one got close to it, the satin was of the commonest kind (not worth ornamenting in any case, and impossible to beautify by reason of its own inherent cheapness), and the roses were being carelessly worked in coarse, straggling stitches, each made to cover as much space as possible. Neither the material nor the work had any durable quality - though perhaps it was just as well that it would not last ; it certainly wasn't worth preserving ! It was merely a bit of showy surface work that was a fraud through and through. The flowers were given a raised appearance by being loosely worked with a very thick, coloured cotton ; and at close quarters the shallowness of it all was only too apparent : one knew instinctively what an impossible rag the whole thing would be after the first cleaning !

I asked the girl what she was

making? "Oh, I don't quite know." she said; "I'm just doing it to fill up my time—one must do *something* at the seaside, you know. Perhaps I shall make it up as a table centre . . . No, I don't suppose there will be any wear in it, but then, I shall be sure to throw it away the moment I am tired of it."

Now here was bad art from every point of view. It was bad work on poor material; it was being done for no definite purpose, the worker merely wanted to kill time; she did not consider it worth her while to put good work into it, because she meant to discard it almost immediately.

Just think what moral harm all that was doing the girl! Think how it indicated a lack of purpose and stability of character, an absence of

any desire to attain to the best, a feeble mental outlook, an inartistic temperament, a disregard of the value of time, and a blunted sense of honesty!

How much better it would have been if that girl had taken a small piece of linen, coarse dowlais if she could afford nothing finer, and have hemstitched the border, or drawn some threads and done a narrow simple piece of drawn-thread work round it, or feather-stitched along a hem and added a piece of crochet, and in this way made a tray-cloth that would have been of definite use when done, that would have stood a fair amount of wear, and would have been good art so far as it went, even though that was not very far.

By so doing, that girl would have been benefit-

A Dutch Interior, showing how artistically Cross-Stitch can be applied to Household Linen.

ing the community, instead of injuring it; she would have been employing her time in producing work that was some use, instead of killing time by producing something worthless and adding yet one more in-artistic item to a world that is over-stocked in that direction already, and doesn't need its eyesight harassed any further.

The lace makers, and em-broiderers, and n e e d l e-workers of past ages set about their tasks in a very different manner. As individuals, they may often have been lacking in general learning, they may have known but little beyond that particular pattern they worked, but what they did, they did well—as well as ever they knew how; and they did it in such a way that their work was not only *worth* preserving, but it possessed lasting qualities that have withstood in some cases, generations of handling and use.

Those workers took a pride in their work; and while many of them did needlecraft for a livelihood, they were artists who worked for more than that mere livelihood. Their hand-work stood to them for something much more dignified than a moment's superficial show, to be thrown away again without hesitation a t t h e caprice of fashion. The needlework of the past was often too beautiful for those who used it to get tired of it; like all real art, it was beautiful for all time; not a bit of clap-trap for the moment only, and y o u w i l l realize this if you study the needle-

> Take your needle, my child, and work at your pattern; it will come out a rose by-and-by. Life is like that—one stitch at a time taken patiently and the pattern will come out all right like the embroidery.
>
> *Oliver Wendell Holmes*

work in the museums in E n g l a n d and on the Continent.

But this does not mean that it was all very elaborate. Some of the old needle-work was quite simple in design. But whether it was plain or ornate, when the workers put into it the best that they were able to do, and worked with a humble sincerity of purpose, they invariably achieved beauti-ful lasting results that we—in this enlightened age—have not been able to im-prove upon, indeed have seldom succeeded in equalling.

I want to urge those of you who have any time to give to needlework to remember that this is as much an art as painting and music and archi-tecture. You can be blunting - or elevating—your artistic sense (and that of other people) by the type of work you produce and display, just as much as by the type of picture you hang upon your wall. You will be lowering your ideals by doing shoddy work and false work, just as you will be raising them by doing work that is thorough and conscientious.

What do I mean by "false work"?

I mean the sort of work that strives by cheap tricks to look like some-thing that it isn't! I recently saw a blouse that a girl had trimmed with some indifferent, m a c h i n e-m a d e coarse cotton insertion, which she had embellished with coloured wool and a little gilt thread run in and out around the pattern. She told me she had done it herself, and asked if

How Needlework Reveals our Aims.

I didn't think it had a rich Oriental effect !! She said she had got the idea from Paris—as though t h a t necessarily stamped it as artistic and desirable !

Sometimes it is very hard to be kind as well as truthful ! I didn't want to hurt her feelings by telling her exactly what I thought : viz., that it utterly vulgarised her blouse and revealed a deplorably " common " streak in her personal taste ! I did the best I could under the circumstances by saying that I thought the blouse material (which was a pretty, simple pattern) didn't need the trimming to set it off.

This serves to show what I mean when I speak of " false work ; " there is a tremendous amount of it about nowadays, and it is all of it rotten. It is having not only a detrimental effect on our national taste, but also on our morals.

The girl who will don badly-machined, ready-made underwear, gaudily trimmed with cheap imitation lace, and garnished with bows of papery ribbon, is not only wasting her money in buying such garments, but is actually pandering to dishonesty, and encouraging herself to tolerate and condone what is false and b a d— hopelessly bad.

The girl who takes a pleasure in making her own things (if she has the time) as nicely as they can be made (whether by machine or by hand), putting fine, even feather-stitching and such-like work into them instead of the " cheap a n d nasty " imitation lace and ribbon, is fostering a love of truth and sincerity, as well as cultivating a se n se of beauty and fitness.

Such matters may seem trivial and of little account to the superficial mind : but they are of grave importance in the formation of character ; and the girl or woman who puts good work, careful work, thorough work, finished work—no matter how simple —into her personal wear and h e r household furnishings, is having an influence for good on her day and generation. She is helping to mould the taste of those who see or handle the things she has made; and above all, she is following the command : " Whatsoever thy hand findeth to do, do it with thy might."

Mosaic Filet Lace.

Mosaic filet lace is a novel idea in fancywork. In this the design is worked with very narrow ribbon somewhat like bébé ribbon, but finer and softer. It is about ⅟₁₆-inch in width and made in all the principal colours, as well as striped and shaded. Use an ordinary darning needle, or a crewel needle, and work the design by running the ribbon in and out through the meshes, in plain darning-

A FLORAL INSET.

stitch. Twice will be sufficient for each row of the meshes, that is just up and down. Cross from one point to another when desirable on the back of the work behind the stitches, running the ribbon, now and then, under one of the strands of the net to be seen behind the part you wish to cross

AN EFFECTIVE DESIGN FOR A CUSHION-COVER.

Lacet Braiding.

Lacet braiding cannot be written of as a new idea, but it may well be revived as an effective means of embroidery. In conjunction with the various stitches used in fancy-work, practically any article can be decorated.

A DECORATIVE MOTIF IN WHITE BRAID WITH FANCY STITCHES.

which are suitable, although not so lasting. Often one can purchase centres and such-like at fancy - work shops with a pattern ready traced upon them. Not every design, however, will suit the lacet braids. Natural groups and sprays of flowers are best avoided, as they mean, in most instances, too many curves, and large flowers require more than a braid outline. A conventional design should therefore be chosen, with fairly close lines.

The lacet braid itself is of French make, and costs 1d. a bundle. The colours in which it can be had are white, red and dark blue, and are best used on a contrast.

As the braid washes, it is as well to have the groundwork of a similar nature. Linen, either white or coloured, is one of the best to use, and there are several kinds of holland-like stuffs for embroidery

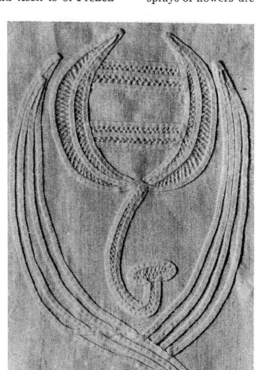

A DESIGN FOR A BAG IN WHITE BRAID WITH HERRING-BONE FILLING.

Curves can be negotiated without puckering the corners, but in all cases where practicable, it is as well to fold the braid over, both sides

104

being alike. Fine cotton (No. 80 for preference) is used to stitch the braid on to the lines of the design, and naturally only small stitches must be made or the braid will not lie close and flat. Sufficient braid to cover a few lines of the design is cut off, and then threaded through from the back to the front of the material, with a needle large enough to take the braid. Then it is sewn down evenly with the fine cotton, until a point is reached where the braid must be taken through to the back of the material, to be brought up again at the nearest point.

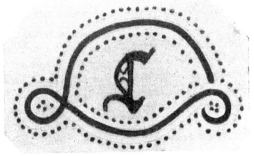

AN INITIAL FRAMED IN RED AND WHITE BRAID AND FRENCH KNOTS.

A CONVENTIONAL DESIGN IN RED BRAID WITH DARNING STITCH.

It is not possible to do all the braiding of a fair-sized piece of work without a break, as the braid is liable to become stringy after it has been pulled through a few times. The ends of the braid must be sewn down neatly on the wrong side of the work.

In cases where the lines of the design come closely together, one row of the braid is laid over the other, and the end finally taken to the back through the same hole.

There is a certain danger of puckering the work when the braid is being sewn across the material when it comes on the cross, but this is practically the only point on which extra care must be taken. All the braiding is done before any embroidery in silk or mercerised

AN END FOR A HUCKABACK TOWEL, INTRODUCING LACET BRAIDING.

Lacet
Braiding.

thread is introduced.

The Design for
a Bag.

Although the braid may well be used alone, yet the addition of some embroidery stitches between the lines is a great improvement. In this, her-ring-boning on a close scale fills up the spaces of the flower and stalk; the leaves are left plain for contrast's sake.

A Decorative
Motif.

Here the braid is used both in straight and curved lines, and the spaces are filled with different stitches.

The lower part is outlined with blanket stitching, and the next small space filled with French knots. Each small square is crossed with 6 threads, fixed in its centre by 1 French knot.

The "bows" and "buckle" are treated the same way in their centres, and in

their outer spaces filled in with Oriental stitch again.

A Framed Initial.

Red and white lacet braids may be employed together for some marking purposes. A "framework" may be made of any shape and size to take 1 or more initials, which could be worked in red or white mercerised cotton. The French knots make a great improvement to the appearance of this form of marking.

An End for a Huckaback
Towel.

Marking in red only cannot be recommended for much more than towels, and huckaback is the best medium on which to work the braid. A central initial and a design on either side is quite sufficient. This is a suggestion which can be easily copied. Darning stitch in red cotton is here used to fill up a few spaces.

Darned Filet Crochet Squares are pretty for inset in linen
or Congress canvas.

Designs in Hedebo Embroidery.

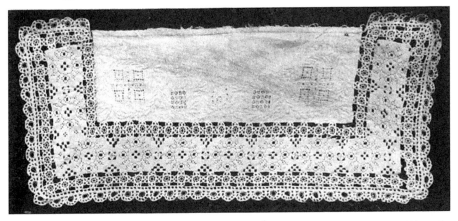

A COLLAR IN HEDEBO EMBROIDERY.

See next page for article on this work.

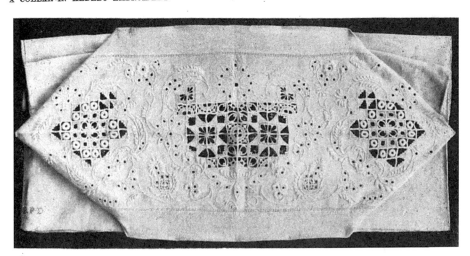

A PILLOW CASE IN HEDEBO EMBROIDERY.

ANOTHER HEDEBO COLLAR FOR UNDERWEAR

The Story of Hedebo Embroidery.

A STOLPE-KLÆDE. USED IN DENMARK
IN PAST YEARS AS WALL HANGINGS.

Hedebo embroidery, one of the most popular forms of Danish needlework, takes its name from the stretch of heath *(hede)* that lies between Copenhagen (Kjoge) and Roskilde in Denmark. From time immemorial the peasantry who lived (live = *bo*) there have spun and woven their own linen from the flax grown on their farms, and their pride in their homemade articles was very great. This led to a desire to further ornament their garments and household linen, and the idea of drawing out some of the threads and rearranging them with a needle and thread was their first attempt at Hedebo stitchery. This probably began as early as the fifteenth century. From these first simple patterns the peasant women of the Hedebo district invented and improved stitches and designs from year to year, until a very high standard of art industry was attained.

Flax played an important part in connection with the love affairs of these people. The peasant lad carved some implement used for the preparing of flax, and presented it to his lady-love as a prelude to the formal proposal. And her first gift to her betrothed was a flaxen shirt with elaborately-wrought collar, front and wristbands. In due course the happy home was made beautiful with hangings of various descriptions in Hedebo work. Over the bedstead was a frieze; between the two doors leading to the kitchen and the passage was a panel. Other items that were the ornaments of every peasant homestead were sham towels and pillow-cases.

These peasant women worked solely

for the love of it, for the embroidery itself was not known or recognised outside their sphere, and was therefore of no market value. So great was the fascination of the stitchery that the workers would often forego a night's rest in order to finish a piece of work.

And even where the husband was averse—as was sometimes the case—to any such "fancy-work," the spell of it was irresistible, and the embroidery was consequently executed clandestinely. History relates of one girl who was told to dig a pit in a field for some stones. When the digging was finished, she sat down to rest for a few minutes. The Hedebo needlework, hidden in her pocket, came out, and she was about to enjoy a little of this pleasanter occupation, when she saw her father coming. To return it to her pocket would only attract his attention to her delinquency. So she hastily flung it into the pit, and covered it with earth, meaning to unearth it as soon as he had disappeared. But she was discovered, and her stern parent, without a word, rolled some stones into the pit and covered them with earth. The long-cherished treasure therefore remained buried for evermore.

The evolution of the Hedebo style is interesting. Up to 1815 the patterns consist of highly conventionalised drawings of flowers and animals on a background of laboriously-wrought drawn-thread work. Then it passes through another phase. The style is still the same—stiff figures—but with the linen itself as background (about 1830). Then the style undergoes a great change.

A STOLPE-KLÆDE. THESE WERE HUNG BETWEEN TWO DOORS IN THE LIVING ROOM.

The Story of Hedebo Embroidery.

A "KNÆ-DUG" IN PAST YEARS THESE WERE USED IN DENMARK AS WALL HANGINGS, IN THE LIVING-ROOM BY THE HEARTH.

The flower motifs become richer and freer; there is also greater variety of stitches in the open-work, which is profusely embellished with chain-stitch embroidery in rows, circles and scrolls; the designs are graceful and the general effect is very lovely. About 1840 Hedebo embroidery reaches its zenith of beauty and perfection; the open-work motifs present a still greater variety of stitches, and the work is, moreover, richly ornamented with garlands of flowers in satin-stitch embroidery. The stitchery of this period is exquisite, both as regards design and execution.

Now follows the decline of the work, showing the artifices used for studying the effect to the detriment of the actual work; for instance, the trick of cutting out instead of drawing the threads, the long loose chain stitches instead of the previous careful ones, lovingly, almost reverently, done. All this contributed to the degradation of the beautiful old art.

Hedebo embroidery was sadly on the wane when some needlework experts decided to revive it. The best Hedebo designs were bought or borrowed and thoroughly examined, much time and money being expended, and "The Society for the Revival of Hedebo Work" was formed. Although it did not possess any capital, various difficulties were overcome by those interested in the work. The Art and Industrial School for Women offered the newly-formed society a flat free of rent, clever artists gave designs, and the Directress of

the Art and Industrial School under-
took the responsibility of leadership.
The Society, whose aim it is to revive
the art and to apply it with a view
to modern requirements, is growing
rapidly, and has now 270 members.
The best forms of Hedebo needlework are taught to its members, and
such work as passes the criticism of
the consulting needlework specialist
is bought by the society. All the work
done by the members is designed by
the artists of the society, and twice
a week members can get advice as to
their patterns. The work of this
society is becoming very well known
both in and out of Denmark, and
it possesses many exquisite designs
from which to study the styles. But
its aim is also to improve the art if
possible, and no effort seems too
great for them so that they attain
this end. And a large collection of

"revived" work, exquisitely designed
and executed, testifies to a result
that must be highly gratifying.

It is an interesting fact that the
majority of the initiators of this
society are men—University Pro-
fessors of the Danish Royal Academy
of Art, and other eminent artists and
architects. It is therefore not surprising that when first-rate needlework
experts took up the work under such
guidance, its delicate beauty should
be restored, for it has been revived
with tenderness for itself as well as
with reverence for its creators—the
women who lived on the Roskilde
Heath.

We are not dealing with the actual
working of Hedebo Embroidery in
this book, as full details of all the
stitches appear in the companion
volume, *The Home Art Book of Fancy
Stitchery*.

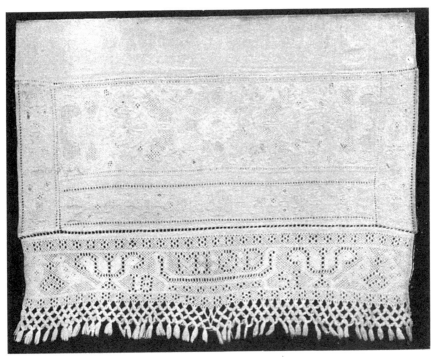

ANOTHER BEAUTIFUL "KNÆ-DUG."

For the Home Dressmaker.

Boning a Bodice Lining.

When making a bone-cased bodice-lining, all the bone-casings should be eased when sewing on, and sewn very strongly down each seam. Also it is much better to use a good quality Prussian bind, or galon, for the bone-casings than a cheap one, as it costs very little more, and will probably last as long as the dress.

Then for this purpose there is really nothing to beat the ready-cased feather-bone, which is sold by the yard at the best drapers, and may be obtained with a silk or satin casing, as well as a cotton casing, either in black or white; the silk or satin-cased feather-bone is especially suitable for evening and best dresses which have a silk or satin bodice-lining. This has only to be stitched on to one side of the turnings of the seam, as closely as possible to the stitching of the seam. After it has been stitched on, and the ends of the stitching tied off and fastened strongly, a tiny piece of the whale-bone (about half an inch) should be cut away from the inside casing, leaving just sufficient of the casing to neaten the end.

Joining the Seams of a Skirt.

When stitching up inside skirt seams, especially those to be pressed open, be very careful to see both edges are quite smooth before tacking up; nothing looks so bad as a puckered seam, with perhaps one edge of the material eased on one side, and the other side quite tight. If care is not

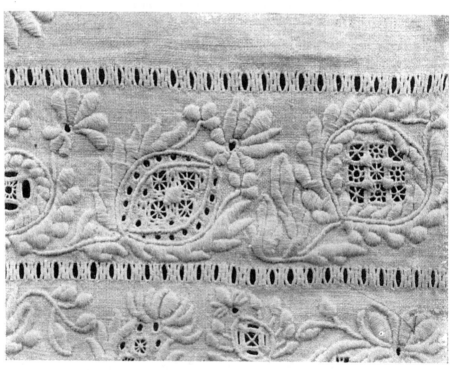

DETAIL OF HEDEBO "STOLPE-KLÆDE" SHOWN ON PAGE 108.

taken before the seam is stitched up, no amount of pressing with the iron afterwards will set it right.

Also be sure the stitching is quite straight. In the case of d a r k materials a rule may be laid down the seam, and a chalk or crayon pencil line marked close to the rule before stitching ; or a piece of ordinary wide tape, held firm at either end with a drawing-pin, would answer the purpose, should any reader not possess a rule long enough. For light materials a tacking may be placed close to the tape instead of a pencil or chalk mark.

Crêpe de Chine, ninon, and all thin flimsy materials are best stitched over paper, as it prevents the seams looking drawn. The paper can be pulled away after the seams or hems are stitched. In fact, all very thin materials look better when stitched with paper underneath them.

Getting an Even Length.

When allowing for the length of a skirt, it is best to take the measurements from the waist to the ground at the front, back, and the hips. Then turn up the skirt to the length you require it off the ground. For instance, if the length should be 42 inches to the ground, and you want a skirt to be 4 inches off the ground, you would turn up the skirt to measure 38 inches, taking 4 inches off the measurements to the ground all round the skirt. Tack up the hem to these measurements, then try on the skirt and see that it is quite even before stitching the hem.

Pressing.

When pressing seams and hems (and when a garment is well pressed it makes all the difference in its appearance), there is no need to use all one's strength, as it were, as I have seen some really good workers try to do.

To Cover Button Moulds.

Before covering button-moulds with the material, the holes of the mould should be filled up with a tiny piece of cotton-wool, pushed in from the back of the mould with the sharp point of the scissors. And if the buttons are to be covered with a very thin material, such as soft silk or satin, they will look, and also wear, better if the mould is covered with a little piece of lining first b e f o r e putting on the outside covering.

When Turning Hems on Thin Materials.

French knots are often used now for finishing hems and fastening pleats, and any reader who does not possess a sewing-machine, I am sure, will find these have a much nicer appearance than hand-hemming in the ordinary way. Also they, of course, make the hem much stronger, especially for thin materials, where hemming stitches would be likely to show more, and for this reason do not have a very firm hold on the second thickness of the material.

Applying Trimmings.

Ribbon, velvet and silk, or mohair braid trimmings are best sewn on by hand with silk, and only one stitch taken at a time, although in some instances the sewing-machine may be used to advantage.

The Foundation Band.

A one-piece dress will feel much more comfortable if the bodice is mounted and sewn on to a foundation-band of petersham, shaped and

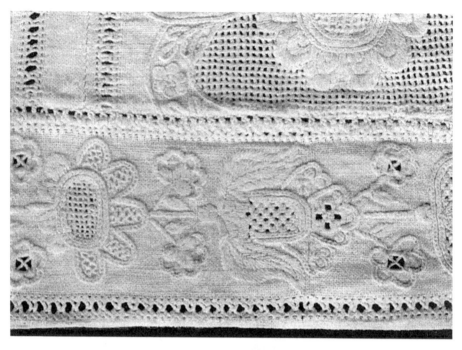

DETAIL OF HEDEBO "KNÆ-DUG" ILLUSTRATED ON PAGE 111.

boned, made to fit the waist, the top of the skirt being sewn to the top of the band. These bands should be fitted to the size of the waist, and the hooks and eyes sewn on before joining them to the dress. If preferred, shaped belting ready boned may be obtained at most drapers, in different widths, for about sixpence per yard.

Fasteners.

The larger press-studs or fasteners, are much better and stronger than the small size fasteners for thick materials, such as serge or cloth, while for thin silk, satin, lace or net, the smaller sizes are more suitable.

Crossway Bands and Pipings.

In making cord pipings, b i a s bands, or flounced trimmings, be sure the material is cut quite on the bias before starting to cut the strips required, or it will spoil the appearance of them, and they will not set properly.

**To Edge Collars
and Cuffs.**

Stitching, in pretty shades of embroidery silk, to correspond with the dress, is a nice finish for a ninon yoke, or collar and cuffs to a dress. For example, a navy blue, w i t h alternate stitches of navy and red, is very pretty, or perhaps three navy stitches and then one red stitch. This is, of course, just a matter of individual taste.

A CATALOG OF SELECTED DOVER
BOOKS IN ALL FIELDS OF INTEREST

CONCERNING THE SPIRITUAL IN ART, Wassily Kandinsky. Pioneering work by father of abstract art. Thoughts on color theory, nature of art. Analysis of earlier masters. 12 illustrations. 80pp. of text. 5⅜ x 8½.   23411-8

ANIMALS: 1,419 Copyright-Free Illustrations of Mammals, Birds, Fish, Insects, etc., Jim Harter (ed.). Clear wood engravings present, in extremely lifelike poses, over 1,000 species of animals. One of the most extensive pictorial sourcebooks of its kind. Captions. Index. 284pp. 9 x 12.   23766-4

CELTIC ART: The Methods of Construction, George Bain. Simple geometric techniques for making Celtic interlacements, spirals, Kells-type initials, animals, humans, etc. Over 500 illustrations. 160pp. 9 x 12. (Available in U.S. only.)   22923-8

AN ATLAS OF ANATOMY FOR ARTISTS, Fritz Schider. Most thorough reference work on art anatomy in the world. Hundreds of illustrations, including selections from works by Vesalius, Leonardo, Goya, Ingres, Michelangelo, others. 593 illustrations. 192pp. 7⅛ x 10¼.   20241-0

CELTIC HAND STROKE-BY-STROKE (Irish Half-Uncial from "The Book of Kells"): An Arthur Baker Calligraphy Manual, Arthur Baker. Complete guide to creating each letter of the alphabet in distinctive Celtic manner. Covers hand position, strokes, pens, inks, paper, more. Illustrated. 48pp. 8¼ x 11.   24336-2

EASY ORIGAMI, John Montroll. Charming collection of 32 projects (hat, cup, pelican, piano, swan, many more) specially designed for the novice origami hobbyist. Clearly illustrated easy-to-follow instructions insure that even beginning papercrafters will achieve successful results. 48pp. 8¼ x 11.   27298-2

THE COMPLETE BOOK OF BIRDHOUSE CONSTRUCTION FOR WOOD-WORKERS, Scott D. Campbell. Detailed instructions, illustrations, tables. Also data on bird habitat and instinct patterns. Bibliography. 3 tables. 63 illustrations in 15 figures. 48pp. 5¼ x 8½.   24407-5

BLOOMINGDALE'S ILLUSTRATED 1886 CATALOG: Fashions, Dry Goods and Housewares, Bloomingdale Brothers. Famed merchants' extremely rare catalog depicting about 1,700 products: clothing, housewares, firearms, dry goods, jewelry, more. Invaluable for dating, identifying vintage items. Also, copyright-free graphics for artists, designers. Co-published with Henry Ford Museum & Greenfield Village. 160pp. 8¼ x 11.   25780-0

HISTORIC COSTUME IN PICTURES, Braun & Schneider. Over 1,450 costumed figures in clearly detailed engravings—from dawn of civilization to end of 19th century. Captions. Many folk costumes. 256pp. 8⅜ x 11¾.   23150-X

PERSPECTIVE FOR ARTISTS, Rex Vicat Cole. Depth, perspective of sky and sea, shadows, much more, not usually covered. 391 diagrams, 81 reproductions of drawings and paintings. 279pp. 5⅜ x 8½. 22487-2

DRAWING THE LIVING FIGURE, Joseph Sheppard. Innovative approach to artistic anatomy focuses on specifics of surface anatomy, rather than muscles and bones. Over 170 drawings of live models in front, back and side views, and in widely varying poses. Accompanying diagrams. 177 illustrations. Introduction. Index. 144pp. 8⅜ x11¼. 26723-7

GOTHIC AND OLD ENGLISH ALPHABETS: 100 Complete Fonts, Dan X. Solo. Add power, elegance to posters, signs, other graphics with 100 stunning copyright-free alphabets: Blackstone, Dolbey, Germania, 97 more–including many lower-case, numerals, punctuation marks. 104pp. 8⅛ x 11. 24695-7

HOW TO DO BEADWORK, Mary White. Fundamental book on craft from simple projects to five-bead chains and woven works. 106 illustrations. 142pp. 5⅜ x 8. 20697-1

THE BOOK OF WOOD CARVING, Charles Marshall Sayers. Finest book for beginners discusses fundamentals and offers 34 designs. "Absolutely first rate . . . well thought out and well executed."–E. J. Tangerman. 118pp. 7¾ x 10⅝. 23654-4

ILLUSTRATED CATALOG OF CIVIL WAR MILITARY GOODS: Union Army Weapons, Insignia, Uniform Accessories, and Other Equipment, Schuyler, Hartley, and Graham. Rare, profusely illustrated 1846 catalog includes Union Army uniform and dress regulations, arms and ammunition, coats, insignia, flags, swords, rifles, etc. 226 illustrations. 160pp. 9 x 12. 24939-5

WOMEN'S FASHIONS OF THE EARLY 1900s: An Unabridged Republication of "New York Fashions, 1909," National Cloak & Suit Co. Rare catalog of mail-order fashions documents women's and children's clothing styles shortly after the turn of the century. Captions offer full descriptions, prices. Invaluable resource for fashion, costume historians. Approximately 725 illustrations. 128pp. 8⅜ x 11¼. 27276-1

THE 1912 AND 1915 GUSTAV STICKLEY FURNITURE CATALOGS, Gustav Stickley. With over 200 detailed illustrations and descriptions, these two catalogs are essential reading and reference materials and identification guides for Stickley furniture. Captions cite materials, dimensions and prices. 112pp. 6½ x 9¼. 26676-1

EARLY AMERICAN LOCOMOTIVES, John H. White, Jr. Finest locomotive engravings from early 19th century: historical (1804–74), main-line (after 1870), special, foreign, etc. 147 plates. 142pp. 11⅜ x 8¼. 22772-3

THE TALL SHIPS OF TODAY IN PHOTOGRAPHS, Frank O. Braynard. Lavishly illustrated tribute to nearly 100 majestic contemporary sailing vessels: Amerigo Vespucci, Clearwater, Constitution, Eagle, Mayflower, Sea Cloud, Victory, many more. Authoritative captions provide statistics, background on each ship. 190 black-and-white photographs and illustrations. Introduction. 128pp. 8⅞ x 11¾. 27163-3

THE STORY OF THE TITANIC AS TOLD BY ITS SURVIVORS, Jack Winocour (ed.). What it was really like. Panic, despair, shocking inefficiency, and a little heroism. More thrilling than any fictional account. 26 illustrations. 320pp. 5⅜ x 8½.
20610-6

FAIRY AND FOLK TALES OF THE IRISH PEASANTRY, William Butler Yeats (ed.). Treasury of 64 tales from the twilight world of Celtic myth and legend: "The Soul Cages," "The Kildare Pooka," "King O'Toole and his Goose," many more. Introduction and Notes by W. B. Yeats. 352pp. 5⅜ x 8½.
26941-8

BUDDHIST MAHAYANA TEXTS, E. B. Cowell and others (eds.). Superb, accurate translations of basic documents in Mahayana Buddhism, highly important in history of religions. The Buddha-karita of Asvaghosha, Larger Sukhavativyuha, more. 448pp. 5⅜ x 8½.
25552-2

ONE TWO THREE . . . INFINITY: Facts and Speculations of Science, George Gamow. Great physicist's fascinating, readable overview of contemporary science: number theory, relativity, fourth dimension, entropy, genes, atomic structure, much more. 128 illustrations. Index. 352pp. 5⅜ x 8½.
25664-2

EXPERIMENTATION AND MEASUREMENT, W. J. Youden. Introductory manual explains laws of measurement in simple terms and offers tips for achieving accuracy and minimizing errors. Mathematics of measurement, use of instruments, experimenting with machines. 1994 edition. Foreword. Preface. Introduction. Epilogue. Selected Readings. Glossary. Index. Tables and figures. 128pp. 5⅜ x 8½.
40451-X

DALÍ ON MODERN ART: The Cuckolds of Antiquated Modern Art, Salvador Dalí. Influential painter skewers modern art and its practitioners. Outrageous evaluations of Picasso, Cézanne, Turner, more. 15 renderings of paintings discussed. 44 calligraphic decorations by Dalí. 96pp. 5⅜ x 8½. (Available in U.S. only.)
29220-7

ANTIQUE PLAYING CARDS: A Pictorial History, Henry René D'Allemagne. Over 900 elaborate, decorative images from rare playing cards (14th–20th centuries): Bacchus, death, dancing dogs, hunting scenes, royal coats of arms, players cheating, much more. 96pp. 9¼ x 12¼.
29265-7

MAKING FURNITURE MASTERPIECES: 30 Projects with Measured Drawings, Franklin H. Gottshall. Step-by-step instructions, illustrations for constructing handsome, useful pieces, among them a Sheraton desk, Chippendale chair, Spanish desk, Queen Anne table and a William and Mary dressing mirror. 224pp. 8⅛ x 11¼.
29338-6

THE FOSSIL BOOK: A Record of Prehistoric Life, Patricia V. Rich et al. Profusely illustrated definitive guide covers everything from single-celled organisms and dinosaurs to birds and mammals and the interplay between climate and man. Over 1,500 illustrations. 760pp. 7½ x 10⅛.
29371-8

Paperbound unless otherwise indicated. Available at your book dealer, online at **www.doverpublications.com**, or by writing to Dept. GI, Dover Publications, Inc., 31 East 2nd Street, Mineola, NY 11501. For current price information or for free catalogues (please indicate field of interest), write to Dover Publications or log on to **www.doverpublications.com** and see every Dover book in print. Dover publishes more than 500 books each year on science, elementary and advanced mathematics, biology, music, art, literary history, social sciences, and other areas.